M000288842

HELL GATE

HELL GATE

A NEXUS OF NEW YORK CITY'S EAST RIVER

Michael Nichols

excelsior editions

AN IMPRINT OF STATE UNIVERSITY OF NEW YORK PRESS
www.sunypress.edu

Published by State University of New York Press, Albany

© 2018 State University of New York

All rights reserved

Printed in the United States of America

No part of this book may be used or reproduced in any manner whatsoever
without written permission. No part of this book may be stored in a retrieval
system or transmitted in any form or by any means including electronic,
electrostatic, magnetic tape, mechanical, photocopying, recording, or
otherwise without the prior permission in writing of the publisher.

Excelsior Editions is an imprint of State University of New York Press.

For information, contact State University of New York Press, Albany, NY
www.sunypress.edu

Library of Congress Cataloging-in-Publication Data

Names: Nichols, Michael, 1951– author.
Title: Hell Gate : a nexus of New York City's east river / Michael Nichols.
Other titles: Hell Gate, a nexus of New York City's east river
Description: Albany, NY : State University of New York Press, [2018] |
    Series: Excelsior editions | Includes bibliographical references.
Identifiers: LCCN 2017053073| ISBN 9781438471402 (pbk. : alk. paper) |
    ISBN 9781438471419 (e-book)
Subjects: LCSH: New York (N.Y.)—Description and travel. | Hell Gate
    (New York, N.Y.) | East River (N.Y.)
Classification: LCC F128.68.H43 N53 2018 | DDC 917.47/104—dc23
    LC record available at https://lccn.loc.gov/2017053073

10   9   8   7   6   5   4   3   2   1

To the fishermen, the mariners, and Tom Maxey—
the *isolatoes*—each his own continent;
and an honorable mention to Salvator R. Tarnmoor

A passage, called by the Dutch settlers of New York, Helle Gat . . .

—*New International Encyclopedia*

These are the true names of the places—but why it has
been thought necessary to name them all, is more than either
you or I can understand. Do you hear anything?
Do you see any change in the water?

—Edgar Allan Poe, "A Descent into the Maelstrom"

Terror enlarges the object, as does joy.

—William Carlos Williams, *In the American Grain*

CONTENTS

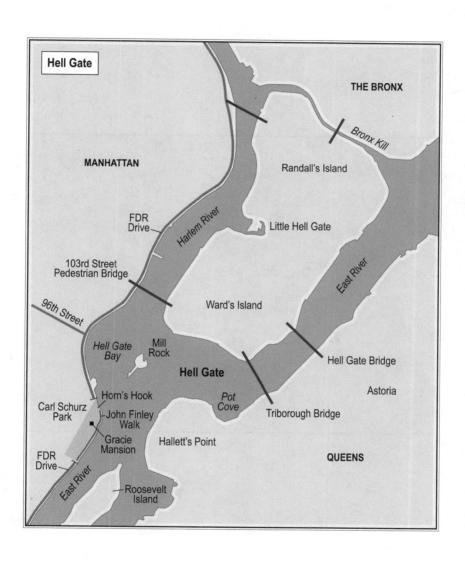

Hell Gate

THE BRONX

MANHATTAN

Bronx Kill

Randall's Island

FDR Drive

Harlem River

Little Hell Gate

103rd Street Pedestrian Bridge

East River

96th Street

Ward's Island

Hell Gate Bay

Mill Rock

Hell Gate

Hell Gate Bridge

Astoria

Horn's Hook

Pot Cove

Carl Schurz Park

John Finley Walk

Triborough Bridge

Gracie Mansion

Hallett's Point

FDR Drive

QUEENS

East River

Roosevelt Island

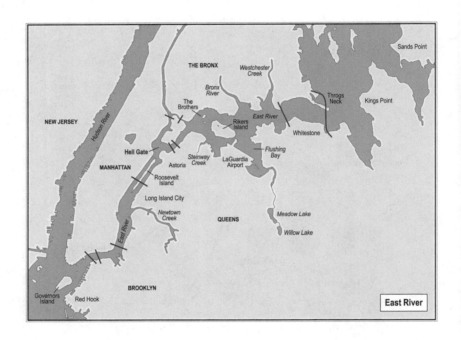

INTRODUCTION

Views of Hell Gate

Panorama

Along the Manhattan side of the East River, just south of Hell Gate, is a long promenade built as a vent for the restless. Built above a short section of FDR Drive, its height allows the same command over water one might have from the deck of a ship: water below, sky above. The promenade is named John Finley Walk, after a local peripatetic who was at one time a professor at City College, later an editor of the *New York Times*, and author of an essay called "Traveling Afoot," in which he had this to say: "And the moral of my whole story is that walking is not only a joy in itself, but that it gives an intimacy with the sacred things and the primal things of earth that are not revealed to those who rush by on wheels." His lasting fame: the promenade itself—*John Finley Walk*—so easy off the tongue that some people think the man's last name is actually "Walk." He was prominent in his day, a friend of Mayor LaGuardia, who upon Finley's death ordered flags at City Hall to be flown at half-mast. He died in 1940, as the promenade's construction was finishing. *How to memorialize him, what to do, what to say?* So LaGuardia named the promenade after him, John Finley, the man who walked.

The walk fronts a small park, named for another favorite son, Carl Schurz, an idyll of thick summery vegetation and winding paths lined with wood benches. Together the park and the walk are a kind of breathing space for those New Yorkers confined to combustibly tight living quarters—which means nearly all of us. The walk and the park are two adjoining rooms: the park is the great room shadowed by tall apartment houses, and the walk is the open deck, high above the water and facing the outdoors. The walk is the perimeter, the margin, and not only does the sky make an appearance here, it is dominant. Its openness is enough to suggest the illusion of escape, as though it were possible to leave the city by putting one's back to it. In warm weather, people are out here by the thousands, walking, parading, talking, enjoying themselves—all out to take in the long views of river and sky, the space and light, and there is plenty enough for all, as though each may have it all, and each may have it all to one's self.

Even in winter, a few hardy souls can be seen on the walk. One can imagine John Finley among them striding his great steps, he who thought nothing of circumambulating Manhattan Island in a day. But most of these walkers don't have Finley's stamina, and indeed some seem to have a hard time breaking city habits. Though they can walk on without confinement and without the distraction of traffic, they indulge in what might be called extended pacing—they walk the length of the promenade, turn back, and when they get back to their starting point, they repeat the cycle. On the Walk, a pacer comes by, again, walking fast. Bald pate, sharp eyes, long gray hair flapping at his nape, the wings of a gull. He is returning. This is his fourth trip by the bench where I'm sitting, but who's counting? He came by a half hour ago and went on. Then he returned. Then he went on. He goes off and . . . *returns* . . . the river flows one way, then the other. He is mumbling something. I lean in to catch his words—folly or wisdom? His mumblings turn out to be the simplest of pleas: *Leave me alone, show some respect . . . I'm not bothering you, am I?*

Ishmael, in *Moby Dick*, asks of the water-gazers: What do they here?

Along the outer edge of the Walk runs an iron rail set into a massive but low embankment of aggregate concrete. The embankment is the perfect height on which to prop one's foot, and the rail is chest high, perfect for leaning into and over and losing yourself to the view beyond—and constructed with such solidity that you can trust the engineering, and be confident the rail will not give way as you dream on. From the rail, you can view the entire sweep of Hell Gate and its environs: to the right, south, the part of the East River separating Manhattan from Roosevelt Island, the Gothic lattice of the Queensborough Bridge in the distance; in front, east, Roosevelt Island and Hallett's Point, in Astoria, Queens, warehouses and low-slung apartment houses crowding the shoreline; northeast and north, the turn into Hell Gate channel, the Triborough and Hell Gate Arch Bridge that span the channel, the southern edge of Ward's Island; and almost the whole of the wide Hell Gate basin west to Mill Rock.

From the rail, all things below are simple: currents flow in and out of Hell Gate, changing direction every six and a half hours or so. The flood current flows southwest to northeast. Later, it reverses: the ebb current starts up from the northeast and runs southwest. If there is no wind at slack tide, the water becomes smooth as slate. You can lean on the rail and watch all this as it happens, should you watch long enough.

I see the coming of the ebb cycle, slow but inevitable: a thin lick of rapid water snaking in from the channel into the calmness of the basin. It heads toward Mill Rock, and continues south. Soon, the whole place will roil.

Later, the roil will calm.

And later, the calm will roil, this time from the opposite direction.

And later . . .

It is a perpetual cycle.

Today we have a chilly morning, but fortunately the wind is down. The sky is clear. I am at the rail, gazing. Current is slow, steady and smooth, not at all raucous, the river almost glassy, mist rising like smoke. Drifting upriver en masse are chunks of ice, maintaining a steady speed and course, each chunk keeping position in relation to the rest. It happens that a single chunk is in front and the rest fall behind to either side, phalanx-like. Military precision. Down the promenade, a woman comes toward me. She looks up, distracted by the ice floe. She stops and goes to the rail to investigate. Her face registers disgust, not fear. She looks around and sees me, a likely target, and asks, "What is that? Pollution?" Urban fears can be gripping, but c'mon, lady. "It's ice," I say. She doesn't look relieved at learning this invasion is a natural phenomenon—because she doesn't believe me. "It's ICE!" I say again, practically shouting. Chunks of ice floating up the city river are less plentiful in her imagination than chunks of debris. She would prefer it to be Styrofoam—floating plastic is something she understands.

She understands the circling arcs of gulls and the lumbering steps of pigeons, and maybe she understands fish. Gulls are here because fish are here, and the garbage scows going up and down the river. Food is plentiful. The gulls in fast flight describe wide circles in the sky. Even in winter they are here, swooping and squawking. They are noisome, obnoxious, and their shit is everywhere.

In the spring, the NYC Parks Department will send out their cleaning crews with scrapers and buckets of water and chemicals to purge the rail of its winter detritus, readying it again for people with elbows and time to kill.

Over the years I've killed a lot of time at this rail, killed even more walking along Hell Gate's edges—the promenades and esplanades up- and down-river—crossing over to its islands, listening, watching, indulging in a kind of movement without itinerary. For me, Hell Gate was not a destination as such, only a convenient place to walk—I lived just a few blocks away. But these walks were not without benefit; along the way, I pocketed into memory many souvenirs: plaques, ruins, oddities, names, stories, impressions, vague sensations, loose facts. . . .

On the map, Hell Gate is at the center of a Y, a nexus of the East River, extending south and northeast, and the Harlem, extending northwest. It is at about the midpoint of the East River, which is not a river but a strait, open to the sea and therefore subject to the sea's crankiness. To the southwest, the river is citified, bulwarked; to the east, it is open and wide on its way to Long Island Sound.

Like the East River's, Hell Gate's boundaries are inexact, its name applied inexactly. Maps suggest two parts: the narrow channel to the northeast, which sluices water through at up to six knots (the "real" Hell Gate); and the wide basin below Ward's Island, which once contained the rocks that broke ships and formed the whirlpools that toyed with them.

Hell Gate's rocky depths are the product of the same glacial forces that formed the entire region, from when the ice sheet that covered much of eastern North America began its retreat a few thousand years ago, leaving hollows, clefts, deep holes. Water from the Atlantic Ocean created Long Island Sound and the East River, found new levels, created new coastlines and islands, their edges becoming coves and inlets, tides turning them to muck on a scheduled basis.

On a large scale, physical forces are predictable: tides are known, winds prevail (generally northeast to southwest, or vice versa), land forms don't change much. But on a smaller scale, predictability breaks down, generalities fizzle. Situations change in minutes: what was easy becomes threatening, or the current that was about to engulf you suddenly ejects you into a placid pool of safe water only a few feet away.

Along Hell Gate are islands and lowlands, shorelines once gashed with coves and inlets that informed the Gate, defined it, nooks of shifting identities as elusive as its name. Land unclaimed until someone claimed it and put it to use: the outwash of creeks becoming fertile terrain for tobacco planters and farms for grazing; country estates built on rocky bluffs that provided a splendid overlook of ships passing through the Gate or else smacking into each other; melancholic islands that penned the sick, the notorious, the insane; depots of stolen goods; graveyards for unknown dead.

Hell Gate is of sea and city. Every so often, the river gives off dimethyl sulfide gas—the "smell of the sea"—the product of marine lowlifes that drifts and diffuses inland, as though it belongs here, which in fact it does, the city being an island before it is a city.

The river water is dark, darker than wine-dark, black at night and a lesser shade of black on sunless days, and noisy when the currents are in full throttle.

Hell Gate is near the geographic center of New York City, which makes it a hole in the midst of a city.

What really set off my explorations was this bit of etymology I found while idling through the pages of the 1939 *WPA Guide to New York*: "The name Hell Gate probably derived from the Dutch *Hellegat* ("beautiful pass") which originally was applied to the whole East River." That the name derived from the Dutch was not unusual; many New York place names come from the Dutch. Every murderous sounding *kill* (Arthur Kill, Kill van Kull, Dutch Kill) comes from Middle Dutch, loosely meaning stream, channel, or creek. Many names were transposed, like *kill*, into English without regard for their Dutch meaning: *Conyne/Konynen Eylandt* (Rabbit Island) became Coney Island; *bouwerij* (farm) became bowery; any name with "hook" (Red, Horns, etc.), from *hoek*, for corner or angle. The English may have wrested New Netherland from the Dutch, but the Dutch presence lingered on through language.

So the transformation from *Hellegat* to Hell Gate seemed obvious given their orthographic similarity, but *beautiful pass*? That the *WPA Guide* delivered this information parenthetically, off the cuff, seemed to suggest a fact that was common knowledge. I trusted (in a Catholic schoolboy kind of way) the book's accuracy, and therefore considered the irony of the fearsome English name deriving not from the fearsomeness of the place itself, but from the idyllic qualities found there by its Dutch discoverers. That those thick and wooded hills surrounding the water, the wild islands, the gentle marshes, the bright and open sky above—heaven—might account for the name.

Not so fast. *Hellegat* had been translated in the other direction as well: "hell hole." Each had synonyms: bright passage, clear passage, passage to hell, whirling gut, and so on, all of which aligned themselves with heaven or hell.

Whether one or the other, or both at the same time—taking some comfort in ambivalence—my view of Hell Gate changed. I began to see everything at Hell Gate, past and present, within a set of contraries or dualities—if not heaven and hell exactly, then secularized versions: idyll/city, paradise/reality. Ordinary physical characteristics fell within new bounds: the currents that flow in and out, the chaos of whirlpools and the calmness of slack, shifting boundaries of land and water. Adriaen Block, the Dutch mariner who named the strait *Hellegat*, had no such cast of mind when he sailed down the East River in 1614. He named it *Hellegat* because it reminded him of one back home—there were, and are, many *Hellegats* in Holland and Belgium. It was the English "Hell Gate" that was localized to the short stretch in middle we know today. The Gate was a dangerous stretch of water, as it is always described, but so are other waters of New York harbor. The striking English name, "Hell Gate," had nevertheless altered the place, not physically but psychically, its name magnifying its reputation, and set forth the Gate's mythic dimensions. Hell Gate, I found, was its own universe, and I set out to trace its cosmology.

Hell Gate is a portal in the literal sense: a place to transit. Ships pass through, no one comes to stay. And with a name invented for allegory, also in the symbolic sense. An entry point for the wretched and the unprepared. Early mariners learned the tricks of the Gate by experience; meanings of names didn't matter. But they respected the place enough to apply names to the parts they feared most. Even the rocks that littered the basin took on identities of their own and entered legend: Frying Pan, the Gridiron, Flood Rock. Then, too, there is a physical resemblance of Hell Gate to Italy's Strait of Messina, between Calabria and Sicily, another narrow and mythic channel, the supposed locus of Scylla and Charybdis (on its Calabrian side, sits the town of Scilla); and the Dardanelles, whose classical name, the Hellespont, recalls the very name of Hellegat. The legendary rocks and whirlpools that upset sailing ships brought to mind the rocks and currents encountered by Odysseus and Jason. I am not alone in this corner: early commentators invoked ancient myths to describe the terrors of Hell Gate, and down to the present day, the names Scylla and Charybdis are given to, of all things, a pair of children's playgrounds, one on each side of the channel.

Even through my reading of books that had little or nothing to do with Hell Gate, I detected—ascribed, perhaps—a northern moodiness to the place, especially on those raw North Atlantic days I spent trouncing about Ward's Island listening to water and wind. In her book *The Flowering of Ireland*, Katharine Scherman draws an image that fit the received ambivalence of Hell Gate's name. St. Brendan the Navigator took off on a long voyage across the Atlantic to search for heaven, and arriving at the volcanic shores of Iceland, thought he had touched the edges of hell. The Irish in fact had a genre of sea literature—*immram*, literally, "oaring around" or "rowing around," voyages that seemed as unstructured as my walks. James Joyce wrote a parody of *The Odyssey* (and the immrama sea tales), in which he relates through the eyes of his Dubliners a catastrophe that took place at the Gate the day before the fictive day of *Ulysses*.

There is something to be said for restlessness, that inability to sit still: it takes you out at all hours and doesn't require much, maybe only a small pack with water and a sandwich. My excursions took me out at all hours, in all seasons, all weather. I made notes, stuffed them into jacket pockets. I retreated into libraries, read books, dictionaries, pored over old maps. It became apparent to me that earlier writers had found the same ambivalence I had found. Much of the literature that bears directly on Hell Gate, what I found of it anyway, exists as a scattering of tangential remarks contained in early New York and maritime histories, much of it by obscure writers and artists (John Flavel Mines, the artist Eliza Greatorex, and her sister, writer Matilda Despard); some of it in lesser-known works of better-known authors (Washington Irving, Edgar Allan Poe); as well as a number of historians and journalists with and without bylines. I culled from them, too. I recall in particular a story by Poe, "A Descent into the Maelstrom," in which an old fisherman tells a young visitor of his terrifying fall into and later ejection from Norway's Moskoe whirlpool—the "Maelstrom"—a swallower of boats. There are obvious parallels to Hell Gate, and the story is shaped something like a Greek drowning myth, beginning on high and penetrating deep into an abyss (Helle falling off the ram into the strait that ultimately bore her name—the Hellespont—made the same arc). But what better suited my purposes was an unterrifying moment before the old man begins his tale, while he and his visitor are sitting on a mountain ledge overlooking the strom: "These are the true names of the places," he tells his visitor, pointing out one by one the islands and rocks far below, "but why it has been thought necessary to name them all, is more than either you or I can understand. Do you hear anything? Do you see any change in the water?" So I walked and listened and watched, pursuing Hell Gate's myth, carrying with me its idyllic/violent name all the while, part of my baggage.

Welcome

Hell Gate: Welcome to New York. How typical of my city that one cannot even enter it without being issued a threat.

CHAPTER 1

Hellegat

First Arrivals

First arrivals are often indirect and imagistic, subject to the direction of the wind at the moment and to misguided expectation. Giovanni da Verrazzano, Italian, sailing for the French, never made it this far in. First land this side of the Atlantic was Cape Fear, and he sailed south keeping close to land. Somewhere off the coast of the Carolinas, he turned his ship, the *Delfina*, around and headed north, continuing past the point of his original arrival. Along the coastline, fires glistened silently in the night. He named this region Arcadia, although historians are not sure exactly where Arcadia was, nor its extent. He passed Chesapeake Bay at night and possibly missed it or saw it and thought its oblique angle meant it did not extend far enough inland to be a passage west. He continued up the coast of Arcadia, and passed Delaware Bay and Cape May. He continued farther and came to a narrow strait between two headlands, one parallel to his direction and the other extending far to the east. He entered the strait, dropped anchor, and went no further. He named the wide bay he found Santa Margarita, after the sister of his patron, Francis I, and the surrounding hills, Angoleme, after the royal family. A gale suddenly rising, he weighed anchor and left the way he came. He continued up the Atlantic coast, along the eastern headland, passing Fire Island, the Hamptons, and Montauk Point. Later, the name Santa Margarita would be forgotten, replaced by Upper New York Bay.

The next year, the Portuguese explorer Estavam Gomez sailed between Newfoundland and Cape May. He may or may not have been in the vicinity of New York Bay. Later still, Jehan Cossin of Dieppe left clues in his log as to his whereabouts, which historians later used to prove he had explored the lower and upper bays of New York. But nothing came of these explorations. Over the next century or so it is probable that other mariners, whalers, and fishermen visited this area—the coast of North America was beginning to receive attention—but the record is scant.

In 1609, another adventurer looking for a passage west, Henry Hudson—English, sailing for the Dutch—entered the bay, and coming upon two outlets on either side of an island, he chose the wider one leading north, and not the narrower one leading east. He sailed a hundred miles up the river, penetrating deep into the wilderness, but a disappointing venture in the end as the river did not lead west, as he had hoped, but petered out at a falls in the middle of nowhere. Whether from selflessness, or from knowing who buttered his bread, Hudson named the river Mauritius, after his patron, Maurits, Prince of Orange. He most likely did not know Verrazzano and Gomez had already christened this place before, and had he known he would not have cared: the Portuguese had no play in this game. Neither did the Italians, nor the French, nor the English (yet). The river would later become known as Hudson's River.

His venture, though, was enough to set the Dutch in motion. Not so many years before, they had established themselves in Asia, the East Indies, following the routes east, on the islands now known as Indonesia, and perhaps this new country and this new river might give them a foothold in the west. Five years after Hudson's voyage, they sent a series of expeditions to North America to get some detail on what Hudson had found. One was captained by a lawyer and merchant named Adriaen Block. Block sailed across the Atlantic and reached a region called Pyebye (Cape Ann, Massachusetts). He turned south and found several capes, bays, rivers, and islands. He coasted through a wide bay between Connecticut and Long Island. He explored rivers, sailing up the Connecticut River to the falls at Middletown, at which point he had to turn back. He continued west and came to a narrow stretch in this bay, filled with small islands and rocks. He made landfall on one of these islands, which were inhabited by a native group called the Manhates, at the mouth of the great river, not far from what is now Vesey Street in lower Manhattan. Block's ship, the *Tyger*, burned after some kind of accident. Its ruined timbers, charred and saturated, were found near Greenwich and Dey Streets in 1906 during the excavations for the Interborough Rapid Transit (IRT) subway

line. What started the fire is not known. Block built another ship using the materials available: the trees all around him on the island. These he felled and shaped into timber. With the help of the natives, who were agreeable to the task, maybe not so much to help him out as to see him out, he constructed a new ship that would take him and his crew home. He named it the *Onrust*. In this *Onrust*, Block sailed east around the lower tip of the island and then up the other side, exiting by way of the same portal he had entered.

At some point in his voyage, in or out, Block named this stretch of water *Hellegat*, supposedly after a branch of the River Scheldt back home. One imagines he often thought of home, especially after a forced winter on an island so far away.

Exactly what it was about this strait that reminded Block of the *Hellegat* at the River Scheldt is not known.

Later, *Hellegat* would be rendered into English as *Hell Gate*.

Onrust is literally *unrest*, or more colloquially, *restless*.

Whirlpit and Whistling

Among the map plates reproduced in I.N. Phelps Stokes's *Iconography of Manhattan Island* is the Figurative Map of 1614, which depicts the coast of North America from New France down to Chesapeake Bay. It is based on information from a variety of sources: Henry Hudson, Jan Cornelisz May, perhaps Samuel de Champlain and surveys of John Smith of Virginia, but mostly Adriaen Block's voyage. According to Stokes, it is the oldest Dutch map of

New Netherland. From a look at the Dutch topographical names drawn on the map, New Netherland extended from northern Virginia through all of New England—England still being a few years away from claiming anything north of Virginia. The full map is broad in scope and lacking in detail, understandable given that most information on the maps of this period were drawn from ships' logs, memory, and a lot of hearsay. Yet to anyone familiar with a contemporary map of the region, the forms along the coastal regions are immediately recognizable: the general lay of the coastline itself; the flexed arm of Cape Cod, the fish shape of Long Island with its tail fins and its head dipping into New York Bay above Sandy Hook.

The map is a trove of information. Indian tribes are named at their places of settlement: the Pequots in Connecticut, Wamapoos in Rhode Island, Aquamachukes in New Jersey, Mohicans straddling the Hudson River, and Nahicans on Long Island (an apparent mistake by the copyists—the tribe was actually the Matowacs). There are oddities attributable to the nascence of the enterprise, among them a large lake identified as the Meer vand Irocoisen, which is near the right place for Narragansett Bay, but is more likely Lake Champlain (it is clearly landlocked and the Iroquois settled around it). Most strange to our ears and eyes, perhaps, are the names given to places we do not associate with the Dutch explorers, particularly places in New England. Massachusetts Bay is the *Noord Zee*, Nantucket Sound is *Zuyder Zee*, Cape Cod is *Staten* or *W'It hoeck*.

Off the western end of Long Island (named *Gebroken landt* on a later map, a name that has been suggested as the origin of "Brooklyn"), is a small, triangular island, almost equilateral in its proportions. The island is peopled by a group identified as the Manhates. And to the east of the island of the Manhates is a wide strait separating it from Long Island and from the mainland, and labeled *Hellegatt*. Thus *Hellegat*, and by extension, Hell Gate, is one of the oldest European names of the region that became New York, older than *Conyne Eylandt*, older than *Spuyten Duyvil*, than *Haarlem, Boswyck*, or *Vlissingen*, older than *Nieuw Amsterdam*.

To Joannes de Laet, the new world's Hellegat held no special terror. He compiled the various reports and maps supplied by returning explorers into his geography, the *New World*. De Laet's narrative, constructed in part from Block's voyages, moves east to west from the New England coast, tracing

Block's route. And in his pages Hellegat is a geographical reference point: "the natives here are called Siwanois, and dwell along the coast [of Connecticut] for eight leagues to the neighborhood of Hellegat." This is not to say the Hellegat was devoid of mythos. De Laet credits Block specifically with the coinage of *Archipelagus*, the file of islands in Long Island Sound just east of the Hellegat, but Hellegat itself he says was "named by our people," as though originating in national discourse. In 1633, De Laet issued a Latin edition of his *New World*, in which his Dutch *Helle Gat* becomes the near equivalent *inferni os* ("hell mouth"). In 1841, George Folsom, translating from the Latin edition, stretched *inferni os* metaphorically into "entrance to the infernal regions." Coupling that with the simple English translation *Hellegat* to "Hell Gate," the infernal image was set. (On a side note, De Laet did not expend many words on Hellegat. More important was the Great [later, Hudson] River, and the Manathan natives whom the out-of-towner De Laet characterized as "a bad race of savages, who have always been very obstinate and unfriendly to our countrymen.")

Not long after Block, other explorers sailed to and through this part of the Eastern seaboard. Exploration increased; traffic grew steadily heavier. To get up and down the coast, many chose the route through the Hellegat, and several left remarks of their travels:

Thomas Dermer, an Englishman exploring the Atlantic coast in 1619, spent enough time here to learn something of the Gate's behavior. Sailing west from Long Island Sound . . .

> . . . through many crooked and straight passages . . . wee found a most dangerous Catwract [Hell Gate] amongst small rockie Ilands, occasioned by two unequall tydes, the one ebbing and flowing two houres before the other: here wee lost an Anchor by the strength of the current, but found it deepe enough: from hence were wee carried in a short space by the tydes swiftnesse [East River] into a great Bay (to us so appearing) [New York Bay] but indeede is broken land, which gaue us light of the Sea.

His Lenape guides, who had committed maps of Hell Gate to memory but none to a page, sketched for Dermer a map in chalk on the lid of a chest to give him an idea of the lay of land and which way to exit to the sea, either east by way of Hell Gate or south by way of the Narrows: "They report the one scarce passable for shoalds, perilous currents, the other no question to be made of." Which one is which is unclear, both sounding bad.

In 1643, John Winthrop writes in his journal a story of divine retribution, near or at Hell Gate:

> Mr. Wither in a vessel of 50 tons, going to Virginia was cast away upon Long Island, with a W.N.W. wind. The company (being about 30) were, most of them, very profane persons, and in their voyage did much to reproach our colony, vowing they would hang, drown, etc., before they would come hither again. Seven were drowned on landing; some got in a small boat to the Dutch plantation, two were killed by Indians, who took all such goods as they left on shore.

In 1663, three gentlemen by the names of Van Ruyven, Van Cortlant, and Lawrence went on a trip to Hartford, taking the expedient way through Hell Gate, of which they speak as a kind of blip:

> In consequence of the strong ebb we could not make much progress by rowing . . . when the ebb was passed we weighed anchor, passed Hellegat at low water, and arrived, by tacking and rowing near Minnewits Island [Mansuring Island, Rye, N.Y.], where we stopped.

This sort of thing goes on for days as they make their way through Long Island Sound to the Fresh (Connecticut) River. They speak of going with the tide and stopping when the tide is against them, possibly the dullest trip through Hell Gate ever recorded, but at least it showed how it should be done.

Jaspar Danckaerts, in 1679, went into considerable detail, writing in his journal a description that reads like a nautical guide:

> The river then runs up northerly to Hellgate, where there is an island, in front of which on the south side are two rocks, covered at high water, and close to the island, besides others which can be easily seen. Hellgate is nothing more than a bend of the river, which, coming up north, turns

thence straight to the east. It is narrow here, and in the middle of the bend or elbow lie several large rocks. On either side it is wider, consequently the current is much stronger in the narrow part; and as it is a bend the water is checked, and made to eddy, and then, striking these rocks, it must make its way to one side or the other, or to both; but it cannot make its way to both, because it is a crooked bay, and therefore it pursues its course until it is stopped on the opposite side of the bay, to which it is driven, so much the more because it encounters these rocks on the way. Now between the rocks there is no current, and behind them it is still; and as the current for the most part is forced from one side, it finds liberty behind these rocks, where it makes a whirlpool. You must therefore be careful not to approach this whirlpool, especially with small vessels, as you will be in danger of being drawn under. It makes such a whirlpit and whistling that you can hear it for a quarter of an hour's distance, but this is when the tide is ebbing, and only, and mostly, when it is running the strongest.

The bend of the river "thence straight to the east" is the bend around Hallett's Point. The rocks are probably the cluster in the middle of the bend called the Middle Reef. Danckaerts kept a meticulous record of his travels up and down the middle Atlantic seaboard, and this description of Hell Gate is the best there is for its day. But the sea was not his calling. He was a preacher. His mission was not geographic knowledge, but to scout locations at which he might establish a colony for his fellow Labadists. His mind was attuned to those whistling whirlpits, and no doubt he meant to call his readers' attention to them.

I'll note here as well that in 1620 the Pilgrims left Holland intending for what was then northern Virginia, now New York—as William Bradford wrote in his *History of Plymouth Plantation*: "to finde some place aboute Hudsons river for their inhabitation." Cape Cod was their first sighting of land, but they continued down the coast until they "fell amongst deangerous shoulds and roring breakers." These may have been Pollock Rip, a shoal off the shore of Eastham, Cape Cod, so dangerous it is said to be the site of most of the shipwrecks off North America. A westerly blew them back to Provincetown. Had they gone on, hugging the shore as they were, they would have continued past Buzzard's Bay, entered Long Island Sound, and thence through the Sound all the way to the East River where they would have discovered Hell Gate for themselves. Wonder would they have thought the place worth a name. The ink inscribing *Hellegat* on the Dutch maps was barely dry at this time.

And yet, what is it about the Hellegat that would warrant a name in the first place? Most places in early New Netherland that were given names, whether by Block or later arrivals, were bodies of water, rivers, islands, peninsulas— outstanding landmarks that mariners would note as they passed through them and claimed. Many of the small rivers on his map were identified by the same stylized squiggles. The "Archipelagus" along the northern coast of Long Island Sound was charted as a neat, double-file of small islands, as if to say, *there are plenty of islands here but we have not yet had the time to survey them for their true position and size.* (Long Island Sound, by the way, may have had its own problems: it's nickname was Devil's Belt.)

The Dutch knew the East River, strictly speaking, was a strait and not a river. Adriaen van der Donck, patroon and patriot who published *A Description of New Netherlands,* an anatomy of his adopted homeland in 1646, noted the fact, and showed little patience for such geographical nicety:

> By some this river is held to be an arm of the sea, or a bay, because it is very wide in some places, and because both ends of the same are connected with, and empty into the ocean. This subilty notwithstanding, we adopt the common opinion and hold it to be a river.

The Dutch were organized, systematic with their toponyms. In his *Description,* Van der Donck does not mention Hellegat by name, but adopts instead the new convention prevalent for rivers: the Noord (North/the Hudson); the Zuydt (South/the Delaware); and the Oost (East/the East), this last either for its position east of the North River or east of New Amsterdam. The North continued to be a commonly used name for that short stretch of the Hudson adjacent to Manhattan, and the East River is the name passed down through the centuries, as if not important enough to be disputed or amended. (Why was there not a West? The Susquehanna might have qualified had the Dutch made it out that far.)

When the English took over in 1664, they kept many of the Dutch and Indian names already inscribed on the land, with at least two exceptions: New Amsterdam and New Netherland both became New York, city and state. Most others were transformed into what sounded or looked like English equivalents. Thus the Dutch *Hellegat* was fixed into English as "Hell Gate," and in so doing its meaning was wrested from its Dutch roots and hellish associations locked into place.

From Daniel Denton's description of New York in 1670:

> For about ten miles from New-York is a place called Hell-Gate, which being a narrow passage, there runneth a violent stream both upon flood and ebb, and in the middle lieth some Islands of Rocks, which the Current sets so violently upon, that it threatens present shipwreck; and upon the Flood is a large Whirlpool, which continually sends forth a hideous roaring, enough to affright any stranger from passing further, and to wait for some Charon to conduct him through; yet to those that are well acquainted little or no danger.

This passage is among the most cited in the literature on Hell Gate. Denton's book, like Van der Donck's, opens with a lay of the land. That Denton's comment on the Gate appears on page two of his twenty-seven-page tract, and never again, indicates he is still just giving his reader an overview of the geographical dimension. Hell Gate is just another node on the map. But it is also worth a comment on its physical character, with its added reference to Charon, and to its noise and fright.

By Denton's time, Hell Gate was no longer the whole of the strait that Block named Hellegat. It had reduced to the point it is today, the bad stretch in the middle—several miles north of "New-York," when New York was still a small city at the southern tip of Manhattan Island. Hellegat may have meant one thing to Block, and something entirely different to the English. Hell Gate and the East River continued to be used almost interchangeably, and even the name East River sometimes appeared on maps as the Sound River, referring to Long Island Sound, an apt if bland name. But it was later New York writers who came to appreciate Hell Gate for its stern and romantic qualities, and played them up in paroxysms of prose.

Names of Fear, Fear of Names

James Fenimore Cooper is a guest of Colonel George Gibbs at the Blackwell house in the Ravenswood section of Queens. He is sitting on the front porch, which offers a splendid view of the East River below. In 1825, the neighborhood is still rural and verdant. In the middle of the river is Blackwell's Island, long and thin, bisecting the river into two channels, and beyond is Manhattan Island, itself rural, even for the few country houses hidden behind the thick brush. While regarding this scene, Cooper sees something that he realizes could become a moment of dramatic irony in a novel, a chase scene, perhaps. Two boats on either side of Blackwell's Island move north in tandem, each obscured from the other by the island of trees between them. What if one was chasing the other and both lost sight of each other? The momentary confusion, the lapse of time. It is a beautiful sight, though, two masts below moving upriver, tied together by the same current, as though space were a liquid through which all objects pass at the same rate, and heading into the turmoil of Hell Gate where space breaks down.

Nineteenth-century romance writers, at least the few who were familiar with New York and its surrounding waters, were fascinated with Hell Gate, and strained to describe what it looked and sounded like, and what it did to the ship you were in, and to you. The very name lighted up their prose. As for the gentlemen Washington Irving and J.F. Cooper, their prose became more intoxicated to the degree their ships of mind homed in on Hell Gate. In *The Water-Witch*, the novel that would ultimately derive from the frail image of two boats sailing up the East River, Cooper permits himself a tedious digression mixing science and psycho-terror in describing the Gate:

> As the size of the estuaries is so great, it is scarcely necessary to explain that the pressure of such wide sheets of water causes the currents, at all the narrow passes, to be exceedingly rapid; since that equal diffusion of the element, which depends on a natural law, must, wherever there is a deficiency of space, be obtained by its velocity. There is, consequently, a quick tide throughout the whole distance between the harbor and Throgmorton [Throgs Neck]; while it is permitted to poetic license to say, that at the narrowest part of the channel, the water darts by the land like an arrow parting from its bow. Owing

to a sudden bend in the course of the stream, which makes two right-angles within a short distance, the dangerous position of many rocks that are visible and more that are not, and the confusion produced by currents, counter-currents, and eddies, this critical pass has received the name of "Hell-Gate." It is memorable for causing many a gentle bosom to palpitate with a terror that is a little exaggerated by the boding name . . .

And from Washington Irving:

. . . a narrow strait, where the current is violently compressed between shouldering promontories, and horribly irritated and perplexed by rocks and shoals. Being at the best of times a very violent, hasty current, it takes these impediments in mighty dudgeon; boiling in whirlpools; brawling and fretting in ripples and breakers; and, in short, indulging in all kinds of wrong-headed paroxysms. At such times, woe to any unlucky vessel that ventures within its clutches. This termagant humour is said to prevail only at half tides.

Termagant humor: overbearing and violent. But at slack tide, there are moments of utter quiet, when the Gate

. . . seems almost to sleep as soundly as an alderman after dinner. It may be compared to an inveterate hard drinker, who is a peaceable fellow enough when he has no liquor at all, or when he has a skin full. . . .

Fishermen, it was said, would use the brief intervals of slack tide to oar out to the rock tables and drop their lines into the chasms below where schools of fish passed through in the deep water. They knew enough, however, to haul their lines and beat it out of there when the time came: ". . . but when half seas over plays the very devil."

But what really lit his lamp was the misplaced propriety of those who could not accept the word "hell" in their personal geographies (or maybe utter it aloud when giving directions). "Hurl Gate" was another variant. Where this name came from is anyone's guess, but it prevailed in eighteenth- and nineteenth-century maps and annals. The mapmaker Matthew Dripps, a sort of Hagstrom of his day, shows in his 1858 map of New York a Hurl Gate ferry between East 86th Street in Manhattan and Astoria, Queens. Woodside Avenue in Queens in fact was known earlier as Hurl Gate Ferry Road—the way to the Queens landing.

Irving, again: splenetic, spewing:

Whereupon out of sheer spleen they denominated it Hellegat (literally Hell Gut) and solemnly gave it over to the devil. This appellation has since been aptly rendered into English by the name of Hell Gate; and into nonsense by the name of Hurl Gate, according to certain foreign intruders who neither understood Dutch nor English.

But maybe *hurl* was not actually a coddling to the faint of heart or soft of head. The journalist and compiler of toponyms Edward M. Ruttenber suggested *hurl* was actually a corruption of the Dutch "warrel[en]," meaning *whirl.* It makes an interesting sidebar, if not a philological fact.

Oaring Around

Daniel Van Pelt:

Some writers feel squeamish about the name, and have informed a less knowing public that "hell" in Dutch means beautiful, and "gate" means a pass, so that this really should be understood as rather a celestial designation than one applying to the opposite place. But Dutch sailors had not much of an eye for beauties of landscape, and the ugly rocks and dangerous eddies which could cause ruin to thousands of vessels in later days would be likely to get from them a very blunt appellation. "Hell" is the German word for clear and bright; but in Dutch the word means exactly what it does in English, and "gat" means a hole. So that if we are thrown back upon what the Dutch word "Hellegat" really signifies, we shall come out worse than ever, and must resign ourselves to the harsh term "Hell-hole."

I got into a discussion one afternoon with a fellow while paddling around Hallett's Cove in a kayak. He was one of the lifeguards patrolling the cove in the event someone should have an accident or drift too far out of the cove and into the channel where the currents pick up. I was a visitor, a first-timer here in a kayak. We paddled within speaking distance, and he started bandying some stray facts about the river. He was a writer, he said, having recently written a book about the East River. In his book he proposed a new name for the East River: Gotham Strait. Interesting name, I thought, for its geophysical accuracy, sort of Batman-ish, but *East River* had long and venerable associations, and it was too late to purge them now. Whatever mystique the East River has, it is of the city: the Bowery Boys, Herbert Asbury and his gang stories, the Brooklyn Bridge, cement shoes, the flue for the oozings and drippings of tanneries, factories, breweries, and refineries that once lined its shores. Soon we were talking about the original Dutch name, *Hellegat*, and its true roots. He casually asserted that *Hellegat* meant bright passage. I countered: "No, it means hell hole."

I think I caught him by surprise, unready to argue and unsure how it is that someone else might have so strong an opinion on so arcane a matter. *Helle*, he said, *helios*, the sun. *Helle*, I said, *hell*. We went back and forth like this, he basing his interpretation on the received opinions of some historians and casual observers, and me basing mine on the received opinions of other historians and casual observers, both of us paddling about each other all the while, the only way to steady ourselves against the buffeting forces of water and wind.

My sources were not entirely casual, and neither were his. He had consulted Dutch speakers. So had I, native Dutch speakers with whom I worked. I figured they, if anyone, would know what Hellegat meant. Unsure of my pronunciation, I wrote the word on a piece of paper. One said it could mean hell hole, yes. Another was more circumspect, looking at the word as though having never seen it. Then I prompted him, bright passage or hell hole? After a moment: "Oh, definitely not bright passage, no way, not possible!"

He was certain what it wasn't, not what it was. So in an attempt to move past quibbling and bobbing, I began a prowl through dictionaries, a fool's errand no doubt, as I don't speak or read a word of Dutch. Nevertheless, if I treaded carefully, I believed I could parse definitions, trace associations, discover patterns. First, there is no entry for *hellegat* itself. It is a compound: *hel* or *helle* plus *gat*. *Gat* appears to mean hole or opening. No quibble there. The *Engels Woordenboek* (modern, Dutch to English) at least revealed a source of the confusion between "bright passage" and "hell hole." *Hel* is a noun that means "hell," and also an adjective that means "bright." English speakers seized on one or the other in their attempt to find an English equivalent. But, of course, *Hellegat* can be traced at least as far back as the seventeenth century (Block's era), probably much further. It appears variously in texts as *helle-gat, hel-gut,* or *hell-gadt.* Also, as Stokes found, *helegate* and *helgatte.* The *Middelnederlandsch Handwoordenboek* (Middle Dutch) links *helle* to *helder* ("clean," bright," "clear"), and also to *steilte* ("precipice"), *kuil* ("pit"), and *diepte* ("deep"). None of this mattered to mariners, of course, nor to Block in particular: he saw something, heard something, smelled something— sensory impressions often being a trigger in conceiving a name.

Unfortunately, Joannes de Laet did not issue an English edition of his *New World*—otherwise things might have been made clearer. Translating *inferni os* into "the entrance to the infernal regions," as Folsom did, made hell the oper-ating metaphor, the primary image today, given its immediacy. Nineteenth-century toponymists found (or invented) various mythic associations to *hel*: from *helios* (sun). Ruttenber suggested that the Dutch origin of *helle* can be traced to the Greek goddess Helle, "as heard in Hellespont, which received its Greek name from Helle, daughter of Athamas, King of Thebes, who, the fable tells us, drowned in passing over it." Or, since languages steal from each other, we can speculate that its origins lay elsewhere, to the north. In Norse mythology, according to Bulfinch, Loki engendered three children, a wolf, a serpent, and his daughter, Hela (Death), who presided over the underworld region also called Hel.

So, give it up. My oaring buddy had another suggestion, a way out of our impasse by giving into it—that *Hellegat* is nothing less than a pun turning on its mutually discordant meanings: it means both heaven and hell, depending on the angle from which you approach the word. And so the name becomes perfectly suited to a paradise of islands geologically configured to generate between them a brutal lick of water. The balladeer Arthur Guiterman, who in the 1920s wrote a sort of epic poem about New York, had the same idea. Guiterman imagined Block at his first encounter with Hell Gate: "De Helle-gat!" the patriotic Block exclaims. (Perhaps Block's timing is right—he arrives when the currents are slack and the river is as gentle as a lake.) Later Dutch sailors aren't so lucky. They arrive when currents are in full throttle against them. Black rock surrounds them, and the whirlpools threaten to take them under. "Hel-gatt," they mutter, a devil's invitation, a warning and a taunt— one can imagine their toothless grins as they approached.

Imaginative stuff, but we don't know. Modern interpretations are more down to earth. Dutch linguist Rob Rentenaar dismisses the religious associations given to *Hellegat,* and notes *hel* or *helle* as noun or adjective. He focuses on topographical elements: "hole," "water bowl," "mouth." In the seventeenth century and depending on the local situation or place, he suggests, "hellegat" most likely meant nothing more than a "low-level pool or swamp-like mouth of a creek," ordinary terrain, earthy, referring neither to heaven nor hell. If so, this could explain the many hellegats in Holland and Belgium. And if so, *Hellegat* had as much to do with the edges of the East River as it did with its turbulent water.

CHAPTER 2

Along the River's Edge

Half-hidden Objects

Reading old maps filled with names that have disappeared and without streets that have yet to be laid down has convinced me of this much: if it were possible to step back in time, one's own city would gradually become a place of increasing amazement, eventually presenting as much strangeness and sense of dislocation as any far-flung Kathmandu would today. Your city, the place you know so well, as it gradually comes undone—oh, yes, here's a place I don't recognize. The familiar ground of asphalt: dissolving. The lines of sight and the constructions by which you orient yourself: shifting, altering, until nothing in front of you is familiar. It's something of a game: finding old markers in the landscape—ephemera forgotten, neglected—and tracing them back to some version of their former life.

Whenever I come to a new place, this question comes to mind, sometimes even before I get my initial bearings: *What was here before?*—as though what is here now is the phantom. The shorelines of Hell Gate, once marshy and craggy, are today, on the Manhattan side at least, as solid as the lines used to represent them on maps: bulwarked, concreted, rip-rapped. Edges distinct, easy to see, and were it not for rails and fences, easy to fall through. Solid land to deep water only inches away. But even here, the constructions and reconstructions along the river did not obliterate everything. Some things are outside one's scope, off the radar, until the sudden flash of recognition that what you've been seeing all along was once something else: to use an enigmatic adjective of Rob Rentenaar's, objects "half-hidden," remains of earlier days, pocketed in corners, their presence never in anyone's way and therefore not worth removing.

In the gap between John Finley Walk and one of the apartment buildings that line the river—that lined the river long before the FDR and the Walk were built—I come across another derelict space of the East River shorefront. About three stories below the Walk, which puts it about level with the river, is what looks like a patio surfaced with crumbling bluestone. The patio is not accessible to the public, presumably not even to the residents of the building. In the wall of the building is a doorway, now encased in concrete, bracketed by squared pillars and topped by a lintel. On the lintel is a frieze pattern filched from the Greeks: waves cresting outward from the center toward both ends. It is the only sign of the deck's former life, inscribed by someone who recognized a good totem for the residents who might strut about the patio wearing a captain's hat. It appears that this patio was once a dock, opening onto the river, for the benefit of the yachting class who lived in the building. The wave motif was no doubt intended to be a totem of the sea. No longer. The frieze faces outward, but outward is now another wall only a few feet away. The deck is forgotten, unseen by any except drifters who happen to peer over the edge of a rail and rediscover it—a walled hole, an unkempt bluestone deck, an impassable door with a lintel inscribed with parting waves, a void at their center.

Vestigial reminders: East 87th Street and East End Avenue: a stone path that winds a bit before straightening and sloping down from street level into a small circular garden below the level of the park, just beyond the arch bridge that connects the two sides above the garden. The garden resembles a bowl or amphitheater: flat, round floor of granite and schist blocks, steep embankments behind a semicircular retaining wall, dense with plantings and shrubbery, canopy of trees above. The embankment is a shroud for the FDR behind it, out of sight, out of earshot. Benches circle in front of the retaining wall. If the Garden of Eden were a hole in the ground, this would be it. At the garden's center, in the center of the circle, is a statue of Peter Pan. A local legend says that pranksters made off one night with Peter Pan, dragged him up to the Walk, and with a mighty heave shoved him over the rail and into the river. A priest happened to be on the Walk, some distance away, and took the pranksters to be murderers disposing of a body. He reported what he had seen to the police. Rescue divers were dispatched, and thanks to the priest's exquisite sense of spatial relationships, they found the statue in the exact spot he said it would be.

This is a place for serious hiding. To some, this is the attraction. People come and sit, then go. Acting troupes sometimes put on Shakespeare comedies, light fare. The acoustics are good. The wind doesn't get down here much. Under intense summer showers, the place floods. On summer afternoons, an intense shower of sunlight. Sticking out vertically from the hump of one of the rocks on the embankment is a thick bar of cast iron, or perhaps bronze, in the shape of a hook, like the top of a coat hanger. It's about eighteen inches in height but hardly noticeable against the camouflage of plantings and rock. Once noticed, however, it is hard to ignore, if only to ponder the mystery of what it is. Once with a purpose, now lost. It is solid: trying to ping it produces only a deadened sound. It is unshakeable, wedged tightly into a crevice and packed with concrete, pockmarked and rough to the touch, but with no sharp edges anywhere after years of weathering.

"Excuse me," I say to one of the park workers, come to sweep up, "What is that hook, do you know?"

He studies it a bit, as though having never seen it before. "Don't know." But now he's curious, and studies it a bit more. "A question mark," he says.

There's my literal answer.

"Maybe to tie up small boats—Captain Hook's hook . . . ha ha . . . there were pirates here!"

Not likely, but possible, I suppose. Consider the elements of the garden's design: the gradual descent from street level, the shrouding of the FDR behind it. This place was the edge of the river, reedy and muddy, a marginal strip between high water and low. Now domesticated, planned rusticity, invoking a neighborhood as it was a century and a half ago when its native wildness was about to be eliminated.

Failing Idylls

On the eastern or "Sound" face of Mannahatta (why do we persist in de-euphonizing the true names?) are some of the most picturesque sites for villas to be found within the limits of Christendom. These localities, however, are neglected—unimproved. The old mansions upon them (principally wooden) are suffered to remain unrepaired, and present a melancholy spectacle of decrepitude. In fact, these magnificent places are doomed. The spirit of Improvement has withered them with its acrid breath. Streets are already "mapped" through them, and they are no longer suburban residences, but "town-lots." In some thirty years every noble cliff will be a pier, and the whole island will be densely desecrated by buildings of brick, with portentous facades of brown-stone, or brown-stonn, as the Gothamites have it.

—Edgar Allan Poe, *Doings of Gotham*, May 14, 1844

Edgar Allan Poe lived in New York on and off several times during his career. When not writing and not badgering editors and not thinking about money, Poe spent time wandering about the city, observing, talking, exploring. While living at the Brennan Farm on the west side, he sat on rocks watching the Hudson. He visited the Receiving Reservoir on 42nd Street and Fifth Avenue (where the main building of the New York Public Library is today) and wrote of the magnificent view afforded from the top of its thick Egyptian-like walls. Poe wrote as if an outsider, which he was to New York, despite his having lived in and out of the city, never quite taking the city into himself—an outsider looking in for the benefit of his readers who were true outsiders.

The passage above followed an outing he took in a rowboat on the East River: "I procured a light skiff," he wrote, "and with the aid of a pair of *sculls*, (as they here term short oars, or paddles) made my way around Blackwell's Island, on a voyage of discovery and exploration." He published the piece in a column he was writing at the time for Columbia (Pa.) *Spy*, "Doings of Gotham." Poe knew what he saw. He is cranky and bothered, mostly by what we do to native language and vestigial landscape. He is remarkably prescient, although some things bear explaining:

By "suburban residences," Poe means the country houses on the east side belonging to the Astors, the Lenoxes, the Primes, the Rhinelanders, the Crugers, the Gracies, and other families—all names of the day, and all federated by business deals, dinner parties, and intermarriage. This was upcountry, and upcountry then as now was the province of the weekender.

By "mapped," Poe is referring to the Commissioners' Plan of 1811, which laid out Manhattan in the gridiron pattern to which the city's future growth would adhere. This far uptown, the grid still exists on paper only, and the map awaits its filling out with actual streets and avenues. But the inexorable uptown advance of the city pushes, and keeps pushing.

By "town lots," he means the neat rectangular parcels being surveyed for the "brown-stonn" townhouses that will eventually be built on them.

And by "the spirit of Improvement . . . with its acrid breath," Poe means that nothing can be left alone.

Possibly he had brother and sister Roderick and Madeleine Usher and their house in mind when he wrote this brief note with his characteristic gloom: "melancholy spectacle of decrepitude," "withered," "doomed." He had written about them only a few years before and perhaps had not fully escaped their fading house. But this is Yorkville, New York, 1844, a small village north of New York City ("New York City" is not yet interchangeable with "Manhattan"), a hamlet in the woods, some distance from the river's edge, near the Boston Post Road, more or less where Third Avenue is today.

In the spring of 1869, the artist Eliza Pratt Greatorex visited this neighborhood with her papers and drawing pens. She was nearly fifty years old, her reputation as a landscape pen-and-ink artist still to be made. She would make it later, with sketches of Oberammergau, Italy, Colorado, and with the sketches she was now doing of New York City, including these neglected houses and cottages overlooking the East River. A book would result, *Old New York: From the Battery to Bloomingdale*, with sketches by Greatorex and accompanying text by her sister, Matilda Despard.

By the time Greatorex arrived, the neighborhood was changing from rural to urban. Yorkville was growing into a middle-class suburb of merchants and bookkeepers, the airy new tenement buildings lining the crosstown streets a welcome relief from the cramped Lower East Side. But that was several blocks inland. Nearer to the East River, Manhattan was a vestigial place, some farms and larger tracts of land owned by the gentry, or what remained of it. Their families were evidently a class in slow diaspora, its aristocratic mores and accoutrements a thing of the past, estates now languishing, failing. It was this vegetative, languishing world that Greatorex elected to capture. Like Poe, she saw a dying paradigm, and what new one might be mapped in its place did not matter.

Every one of Greatorex's drawings of this neighborhood has one thing in common: a house as the focal point, but so completely surrounded by vegetation that it is not the house that matters but the captivity of the house. Her drawings are like those of the nineteenth-century explorer-artists who intended to describe exotic lands as precisely and scientifically as possible, but which today look nothing less than Romantic. Her landscapes work in tandem with Poe's lament, also his House of Usher. Nowhere are people. Not that people didn't exist.

While Greatorex was sketching the Astor house, a curious bystander happened by, an old Scot, presumably a servant of the house. He spoke to her of the bygone days when Mr. Astor was still alive and how he maintained "the good and pleasant fashions of the olden times. There were many servants in the house, and fires of blazing hickory were kept even in summer—a wise precaution against country chill and damp." But now the hickory had run out, or maybe just those who would tend the fire. In 1873, Mr. Astor's house would be torn down. There was no point in letting it linger on, lest it fall and become part of the vegetation.

At East 86th Street, just a block north of the Peter Pan Garden is another path that extends across Carl Schurz Park. It shares some general characteristics with the first, only grander, a centerpiece to the park: a double path on either side of an arcade of trees leading to a small plaza with a double staircase leading up to John Finley Walk. It, too, slopes down, though the slope is barely perceptible—unless, I suppose, you are on wheels (Boy on a skateboard: "I don't want to skate up the hill." Father: "What hill?"). Here too, Greatorex provides some pictorial documentation of a segment of life at Hell Gate. Looking down a rutted East 86th Street toward the East River, she used the arching branches of trees and the rock walls to create a kind of gyred tunnel. At the end, in a small space of light, was the Hell Gate Ferry Hotel, a stop for wayfarers and passers-through from Long Island across the river. In its day, about twenty years before Greatorex arrived, when it was run by a Mr. Dunlop, the place was something of a resort, if Dunlop's advertising can be believed:

An obliging host, beautiful summer retreat, refreshments of the first quality with horses and pleasure wagons to let. Also, boats and tackle for fishing, renders this spot second to none in the vicinity of New York City. Murphy's stage, every fifteen minutes to City Hall, for six cents.

By the time Greatorex arrived, there was not much activity for a hotel. In fact, the place seemed to be in ruins, perhaps the oldest house she might come upon. It was built of heavy stone, its sills and ledges of lighter brownstone. Inside, the place gave the appearance of a once comfortable dwelling, roomy, with small panes of glass set in windows and doors. A rambling balcony remained, affording a wide view of the river, if one can trust to step out on it. Should travelers come by wanting to summon the ferry, they needed only to alert the ferryman by blowing a loud signal through a conch shell. In most of her other works, Greatorex centers her frame with a house. In Hell Gate Ferry Hotel, the hotel is a little off center, the true focus being the bright hole of light through the trees at the end of the sloping street, leading the viewer's eye to the river.

The Mayor's House

When in the 1940s city officials decided the mayor should have an official residence, Mayor LaGuardia was first shown a nineteenth-century neo-French Gothic chateau: seventy-five rooms, mansard roof, ornate accoutrement, and New York City's best address—Riverside Drive. Fiorello H. LaGuardia, the mayor of the people who talked up to President Roosevelt and who read the funnies on the radio to children during the newspaper strike of 1940, took one look and said, "What! Me in that?" Robert Moses secured for LaGuardia (and all mayors hence) a house crosstown, on the east side, something smaller, more humble, more him.

Of all houses that Greatorex sketched in this neighborhood, one remains. At the northern corner of Carl Schurz Park is Gracie Mansion—legacy of the merchant Archibald Gracie and now the official home to the mayor of the City of New York. The knoll it sits on is Horns Hook, a natural observation point for the Gate, the riverside curving to the west opening the whole of the Gate in panorama. The view was known to the Dutch, to Sybout Claasen, a carpenter, who received this land in 1646 in settlement of a disputed debt. He named it for his native town, Hoorn, in Holland, possibly for patriotic reasons, possibly out of nostalgia for the way this corner of Manhattan Island jutted into the East River the way Hoorn jutted into Zuider Zee. (Cape Horn, the southern tip of South America, is another place said to be named after the town.) Gracie Mansion looms darkly behind a red brick wall and beneath the spreading branches of the London planes. On the brick wall in front, next to the guardhouse always manned by a policeman, a plaque reads:

> Landmarks of New York. Gracie Mansion. Built about 1799 on the site of a revolutionary fort as the country house of Archibald Gracie, Scottish Merchant, this colonial structure was restored in 1927 under the supervision of the Park Department. From 1923 to 1932 it housed the Museum of the City of New York. It is now the official residence of the mayor of New York. Plaque erected 1960 by The New York Community Trust.

Mayors speak of budgets and let the furniture do the history. That Gracie Mansion has survived this long can be credited to its being a shape-shifter. History knows Archibald Gracie more for his house than for him. He was hardworking, industrious, scrupulous, and successful until President Jefferson's embargo in 1807. Then it was all downhill. To pay off his debts, Gracie sold the house in 1823 to Joseph Foulkes, who later sold it to Noah Wheaton, whose family kept it until his death in 1896. The family sold it to the City of New York, and not knowing what to do with it, the City of New York allowed it to languish, but never to the point that it was beyond rescue. It served time, variously as an ice cream parlor, a public bathroom, and the Museum of the City of New York. In its rooms today are fine old Georgian furniture, paintings, carpets, and on a mantle some cannon shot from the days when this site was a Revolutionary battlement.

Gracie wasn't the first to build on this knoll. In 1770, Jacob Walton purchased eleven acres here to build for himself and his family a weekend retreat, far from the mean business streets of the city. According to Charles King, it was an attractive place:

> The elevated plateau, covered with thick woods and lesser vegetation, the ocean breezes, which sweep over it, following the rising and falling tides and its proximity to the swift, salt river, it seems a spot, marked by nature itself.

Walton was from a prominent family. His grandfather William had early on purchased land on the East River on which he built shipyards. He must have been quite the adventurous sort. He was known as Boss Walton, and also as Captain, as he sailed his own ships to the West Indies and along the Spanish Main. Imagine today's airline president piloting his company's planes. Jacob's generation was more settled, business-like, married to responsibility and good sense. The firm he ran with his brother, also William, was said to be the largest insurance underwriting business in the city. Walton married well, to Polly Cruger, the daughter of Henry Cruger, a member of the provincial assembly and the ministerial party. For a few years the family lived in peace, but it was Walton's bad timing to build his retreat just as a world war was breaking out.

Strategists knew the place, too. General Washington, looking at the map, decided he needed this promontory, and as General Lee was in charge in these parts, Washington ordered Lee to take it. Which he did. Walton, Loyalist, was expelled, the house turned into a bivouac for the rebels who were to man the redoubt down the hill. One can imagine the turn: in September, 1776, the British fired at the redoubt from across the river, at Hallett's Point. Their missiles also hit the Loyalist's house, burning it to its foundation. Supposedly, Walton had dug a tunnel from his house down the river's edge, an escape hatch, found a century or so later when they were building Carl Schurz Park. The tunnel no longer exists, a hole being destroyed by addition.

The site is still attractive, with new growth as thick as in Gracie's day, and a granite wall along the eastern edge of the grounds acquiring a patina after decades of exposure to the soot and rain and Hell Gate's sea-salt spray. If only I could climb those walls and sneak onto the lawn, lie down, stretch out and watch the evening sky. Maybe the mayor, bored with the official festivities going on inside, will come out to smoke a cigar. And I'll invite him over to my spot far down on the lawn. "Mister Mayor, I confess, I am going to run against you in the next election, but it has nothing to do with your record and your accomplishments, meager though they are. It is only because the mayor gets to live in a house with a lawn and a porch that has a fine view of Hell Gate and the smell of the Atlantic sweeping through." The mayor replies, wearily, "That's a better reason than most."

But to hell with politics.

Strange that mayors, who can get away with saying "My city," never say it. It is always "Our city," with that careful inclusion of the body politick. But I'll bet more than one mayor has stepped out onto the yard of this citified country house on some languorous summer evening—and smelling the sea, and taking in the view of the wide Hell Gate, the twinkling lights of the bridges, the great buildings upriver and down, the barges plying the water, the gulls, the sky framed by a grove of oak and London plane, the evening's descent—I'll bet more than one mayor has said to himself: *My city*.

Having breathed in enough of that sea-salt air, the mayor rises and ambles back up the hill to his house, the porch light having been left on to guide him, praying that the city will get through the night without the need for political intervention.

A Place with Chairs

North of Horns Hook, at about East 89th Street, John Finley Walk descends down the side of the knoll on which Gracie Mansion is situated to just above river level, and curves slightly to the west following the river's shoreline. Now I come to different territory. The bluffs give out, the land flattens. No reminders here of defunct aristocracy. No Poe, no Greatorex to record the scenery. At the time they were making their comments on the failing houses and the new suburbs, this was a swamp. Somewhere along here the Walk loses its name John Finley and somewhere before 96th Street becomes the East River Esplanade. Now I am on a narrow pedestrian path of asphalt squeezed between the river and the FDR, once known as East River Drive, a name still carved in stone above the entrance to the tunnel that plumbs through the knoll. The unceasing flow of traffic produces a rhythmless oceanic din as one side hurtles downtown where it will spill into Manhattan's streets and the other uptown where it will fan out to the Bronx, New England, Long Island. Jutting into the river on the right, as you head north, is the old fireboat pier, one of the few piers built in Manhattan for the purpose, and now recon-ditioned for the NY Waterway ferries, one of the last piers of any purpose remaining along this stretch of the shoreline. On the left, across the FDR, are high-rise apartment buildings ("stupendous river views"), pleasant gar-den apartments with dark inner courtyards, and a massive parabolic-shaped concrete structure, once the administration building for an asphalt plant that has since found re-use as a recreation center. The George and Annette Mur-phy Center is the name inscribed on its walls, owing to their largesse in its preservation, but "Parabola" says what it is. It is a landmark in the legal sense and the geographic—a thing preserved by ordinance and a thing to bring one to one's true bearing, a futuristic presence too otherworldly for its mun-dane setting. At night especially, when its parabolic face is illuminated and the sky surrounding it is empty and dark, it is a form worthy of De Chirico's metaphysical dream cities.

I walk north. The river begins to widen, indenting and cutting a cove into the eastern side of Manhattan, about the island's midsection. It has, or had, a name: Hell Gate Bay, when it was a real bay, cutting deeper into Manhattan's side (almost to Second Avenue) and blending with the marshes and the out-flows of creeks whose sources were amid the rock that forms the heights of Manhattan farther west. Now we get closer to Hell Gate. The closer one gets to the hell hole, the more it becomes a bright passage. And yet it is a dreary flatland. The currents stay far out in the river. Nearer to shore, Hell Gate Bay is a sargasso of river crap and garbage. When the tide is slack, especially.

I walk on, continuing on the path of inlaid hexagonal asphalt tiles lined with flower gardens and wooden benches, the answer to the question of what to do with the city's shoreline, how to package it into something enticing and lively. Runners run, walkers walk, cyclists cycle. Fishermen hold out. Even picnickers spread blankets, taking in the river views as well as the traffic's din at full volume. Its industrial past is not completely lost. Remnants remain: the Parabola building and the old fireboat pier, the old Sanitation pier, where garbage trucks dump their load into barges for cartage elsewhere, and now being demolished and replaced with a larger and more technologically advanced version.

Farther up the west channel, where the East River becomes the Harlem, was once another pier, this one belonging to an outfit called the Washburn Wire Company, one of the last of many piers that once occupied this stretch of the river above Hell Gate Bay. The Washburn complex consisted of a factory on the land side of the FDR, the pier on the river side, and a covered bridge over the highway to connect them. I first found the Washburn on an earlier excursion, abandoned and barely sustainable even then. The holes in its roof were a skylight letting in streams of daylight. I took a few steps inside, taking care to tread lightly. There were cracks in the floor, places where sections of the floor were missing entirely, exposing the black, lapping water underneath. I took another step and collapsed a board, sending it into the river, almost falling in myself, saving myself only because I tread lightly.

I made return trips. At night the place had a sinister aspect, a deep and endless cavern in the dark except for shards of glass glistening in the moonlight. I imagined colonies of rodents, but I saw none. I detected no human presence nor signs of any, no bedding and such, no tins of encrusted food. But here were possibilities for the modern vagabond: a way station; a place to ponder ruination and abandonment; or a detective show: the place where in the opening scene someone finds the body. One could imagine doing in an enemy or betrayer and making a clean getaway before the television crews show up; or as the last home of the suicide who has found a place to make a tidy escape—a slip through the cracks won't make a splash, and the current carries you home.

But the Washburn now seems misplaced. I come to a new pier, recently refurbished with a wooden boardwalk, rails, a roof over the center length. Fishermen are the main users, along with a few cyclists on respite. For a moment I think this might be the Washburn, but it's not in the right place, the surroundings that I remember are displaced, the angles of streets and neighboring buildings incorrect when measured against memory. Further on, I come to a grid of pilings dug into the shallow riverbed. Across the FDR was an empty lot. In this place, things felt aligned: *this* was the Washburn, no factory, no overhead bridge, the only remnant of it being those submerged pilings, a shadowy presence barely visible under the surface of a low tide.

Along the esplanade, everyone is acquiesced to urban noise. A man seated on a bench and dressed in orange pants tries to sell his bicycle: "Ten speed, ten dollars." Nice alliteration, but did I hear that right? "Ten speed, ten dollars." I guess I did. You read what you want into the things that you see and hear. Two children at the rail, trying to spook one another: "Water rats run along the rocks, they swim," says the first. "No!" yells the other, "they drown, they . . . DROWN!" "A water rat once came up here," says the first. "It was THIS big." The usual parade of bikers and runners, attracted by the ease of movement along the flat path, and who believe they own it, given the squawking they do at all who get in their way.

And if one more cyclist rings his little bell at me . . .

I happened by a fisherman with his young son at the moment he was reeling in a small, whitish, pinkish, fleshy-looking thing. It swung near my face, startling me for being so close and so alien. It looked like a white tongue. "What is it?" I asked. "A clam," he said. "Are you going to eat that?" "Probably not." He was suddenly cautious, almost shy. His son came around to eye me, as though to protect his father. He must have been about nine. I asked the fisherman what he goes for. "Flounder and eels." He wrenched the clam from its hook and threw it back into the water. It was later that Marco, a buddy of mine who fishes himself, cleared up the mystery for me: "It was bait," Marco said, without hesitation. "He was probably going for striped bass." "But he threw it back in the water," I said. "Maybe he thought you were going to give him a ticket. You were asking too many questions." "I asked him what he was fishing for," I said. "That's too many questions," said Marco.

"That could be," I said. In that context, that could be. There are rules regarding what fishermen can and can't do, and I had wandered in at the wrong moment. No wonder the kid was trying to protect his old man.

Marco fishes up and down the East River, along the shores of Upper New York Bay. He goes for bass and porgies, but really anything that bites. He allows that he has caught young porgies and breakfasted on them, strictly for the melt-in-your-mouth quality of their meat. At Hell Gate he practices his

craft somewhere along the Astoria waterfront, at "a place with chairs." I do
not press him for the exact location, not that he's being secretive, but more for
leaving intact the mystery of the phrase, a place apart from common places,
and in which someone has spread a gaggle of chairs, empty most of time, until
the hour when someone comes to sit, bait his hook, throw his line. One sits
and lets the flow of water become the flow of mind. The catch is the product,
but it is not the main idea; it is rather an adjunct to process and reverie.

Further up along the Esplanade are more fishermen, some are alone, others
in groups of two or three. They are a mute bunch and call to mind Melville's
portrait of harpooners aboard the *Pequod* in *Moby Dick*:

> Isolatoes too, I call such, not acknowledging the common continent of
> men, but each Isolato living on a separate continent of his own. Yet now,
> federated along one keel . . .

Each a continent to himself, and each one a man of skill and workman-
ship, perfecting those skills and loyal to the work, not necessarily to any captain. They barely attend their lines, propping their poles along the rail and
then retreat to the benches where they sit and wait or watch for signs of a
fish. A group of card players doubling as fishermen play pinochle on a folding
card table. They have brought their radios with them, and still the blare is not
enough to drown out the traffic din. A concrete abutment topped with a short
iron rail is all that separates them from the hurtling cars, a distance of not
more than six feet. How brave, but who can hear himself think? The players,
evidently, each one able to concentrate on the cards in hand, and to shut out
all distraction. They are fishermen, they have learned from fishing patience
and their habits of concentration.

Mottos:

"It's not about the fish; it's about the escape."

The necessity of the city: build a bulwark, and let drown what remains
outside.

When you want to be alone, find a ship or an island . . . if not that, a margin,
an edge . . . or else a firm bench. It's not unusual to find chairs and tables left
behind by fishermen. Just yesterday, I happened on a small collection: two
folding chairs, a desk chair on wheels, and a leather ottoman.

Coming toward me are two boys carrying an ice chest, each holding on to the handle at either end. The older one swings position to step directly into my way. With a heavy cooler in his hand he cannot be a mugger, maybe a salesman, a slight upgrade in my book. "Water, sir?" asks the older one. It's a warm day. "The dollar size," I say. He and his friend put down the chest and open its lid. "They're all the dollar size, sir." I reach into my wallet and pull out a single. Current economics in the city are perfect in this way—all incidentals sold in the open markets of street, subway, or river walk are transacted at one dollar per. The transaction being made, I open the bottle and take a swig, perhaps a gill or two, then stash the bottle in my satchel and proceed. I feel . . . *stoked* . . . *provisioned* . . . all the more reason that I begin to think: I am getting too old for all this walking around, ought to settle down, find myself a bench of good wood pinned to the concrete, where I can sit and drop a line.

Low, Swampy, Creek Mouths

Topography is not much in mind when I walk the streets of Manhattan, running my usual errands—grocery, bank, dry cleaners. The object is to get to a place, execute my business, and leave. The low inclines of street and avenue do not produce enough of a physical challenge to make me aware of them, are not enough to remind me that Manhattan is an island with hills and creeks. Avenues run twelve miles up and down the island with Euclidean precision; streets cross them, river to river, with equal precision, their intersections forming perfect 90-degree angles—hundreds of them arranged in neat rectangles across Manhattan—all of this the Grid Plan of 1811 made real, the plan that sent streets straight up hills instead of around them, sent creeks underground and out of the way. But not all of Manhattan could be so conditioned. Far uptown, the hills are steep enough that streets had to angle around their base. Far downtown, some streets were laid out to follow the river's edge. Some sections of the island still make the old topography obvious: at river edges, for instance, which still curve and which in places along their length are lined with bluffs, or where level flats of ground extend blocks inland. Here, for instance, at the sinuous curve of Hell Gate Bay until it was encroached with enough landfill to make it but a minor indent in the midsection of the island.

Having learned that *Hellegat* may refer to swamps and creeks, I see them everywhere under the skin of Manhattan, in every flatland a possible repossession of marsh and water. I have a topographic map of Manhattan published in 1909 that explains this flatland: "Manhattan Island, 1783, At the Close of the Revolution," published, maybe drawn, by Townsend Maccoun, a name completely unfamiliar to me, but evidently an accomplished author of geographical charts of the United States, Europe, and the Holy Land. His map of Manhattan shows the island's natural features at a time when they meant something: when travelers had to climb hills, traverse meadows and woodlands, ford creeks and kills, dock their boats in coves along a raggedy shoreline. At the bottom of Manhattan, at the Battery, there was a city; at the top there was Spuyten Duyvil, twisting and looping, penetrating into a soft corner of the Bronx. Overlaying the terrain are thin red lines showing the 1909 street patterns, avenues and representative crosstown streets. At the edges of the island, drawn in light blue, is the waterfront of 1909—landfill, docks, and piers. Thus the map shows a double past: the island as it was before it was a city, and the city as it was in 1909, now so out of date as to be itself a historical view. In the loins of Manhattan Island, east of Hell Gate, a set of sinewy topographic lines depicts a flat plain between 90th and about 110th Streets, and extending from the river back to Third Avenue. Threading this plain are darker blue lines denoting interior waters—narrow gullies, creeks, and kills that begin in the high hills of Manhattan's west side and trickle down, widening and slowing as they gather into pools and ponds until they all join in an alluvial, boggy outwash whose edge is indistinguishable from the bays and coves along the shores of the East and Harlem Rivers into which these waters ultimately empty. I counted thirty-four of these outlets on the East River between the Battery and 125th Street.

The thickest of the blue lines on my 1909 map is called Mill Creek, which unsurprisingly is a common name for any creek with a mill. The creek's source was on the west side near 125th Street, west of what is now Morningside Park, and wended its way downhill toward the east. By the time it reached the East River, it was as wide as a modern city block. It was said to be navigable several blocks inland. Mill Creek is a lesson in toponymic fluidity and informality. Another of its names is Harlem Creek, for its location; also, Benson's Creek, for the fellow who built the mill; and Benson's Mill Creek, for the fellow and his mill.

Again, I think of Adriaen Block, passing by the vast swamp near the whirl-pool, and Rob Rentenaar's description of low, swampy, creek mouths. Accord-ing to John Flavel Mines, who lived and wrote here, the Dutch gave these flats a name: *Conykeekst*, home of the rabbit, and they found its rich soil easy to till. "The mind of the Hollander," Mines writes, "was instinctively drawn to what the early colonists called the flats of the Island of Manhattan, and the region was all the more attractive because it was bordered by salt meadows traversed at many points by creeks and kills." Using the creeks and kills to their advan-tage, the Dutch built a dam, mills, a tavern. Bogs were drained; houses and farms sprang up. Much later, the city built itself up here on this reclaimed ground. Kills were straightened and driven underground through pipes used to eject waste and water. The pipes still exist below the streets, conveniently out of sight. During Hurricane Sandy, cellars flooded, the waters coming from underneath meeting the waters spilling over the bulwarks of the East River, a reunification of sorts, the progress of technology notwithstanding.

John Flavel Mines, lawyer, journalist, nostalgiac: you can find his work on the internet, posted piecemeal, often in short extracts, sometimes under the pseudonym he invented for himself, "Felix Oldboy," or as often as not, anonymously. He wrote of this Conykeekst and Hell Gate neighborhood in the 1890s, as it was sliding from rural into citification. In his youth, the 1860s, Mines had spent a summer or two in a house at Horns Hook, a house that from his description of its porch and frontal aspect sounds suspiciously like Gracie Mansion. Like most nostalgists, he is part sentimentalist, part curmudgeon. His Felix Oldboy persona is fitting for one who recreates a pas-toral district harking back to a time when the city was barely touched by the works of man, or so he remembers. *My Summer Acre* he calls it, the place and the book:

My summer acre fronts upon the East River, near the spot where the waters of Hell Gate begin to seethe and swirl. Standing on the little bluff in which its garden ends, and towards which its velvety lawn descends from the back porch, one can see the rarest and loveliest of pictures. Across and up the river where Pot Rock once made the waters boil and the Frying Pan was a terror to navigators; where Flood Rock is alternately submerged and exposed by the tides; where the Hog's Back and Nigger's Head yet wreck an occasional vessel; where the shaded river road of Astoria allows rare glimpses of stately mansions between the trees, and the green ramparts of Ward's Island are wondrous pleasant to the eye and hide other lovely islands beyond that are fruitful of legends as of lobsters—are stretches of scenery than which there is nothing more beautiful on the Atlantic coast line. Back of me and on either hand may be heard the coarse melody of the hand-organ, the strident shriek of steam, the shouts of children at play in the streets, the ceaseless undertone of wagon and incessant hum of labor, and the puff of steamboat and clatter of tug may be heard upon the waters; but the sunshine turns the silver of the breakers upon the rocks to gold, the shadows of overhanging trees mirror themselves in the quiet waters of tiny bays, the little hills are clothed with beauty as with a garment, and I have enough of imagination left to fancy myself in Arcadia.

City and Eden; paradise versus reality. Curious imagery: the bucolic images are mostly visual, rare and lovely pictures of lawns, trees, but the city images are for the most part aural, not yet in sight. In other words, the city is creeping up *behind* him, mostly out of sight, but within earshot: shouts, shrieks, undertones, huffing, puffing, an organ grinder (the emigre Eye-talians?). Hell Gate, we might note, despite its terrors, is part of paradise, a place not so terrifying, maybe, but still capable of wrecking the ill-prepared ship. "It has been a disappointment to me," Mines writes, "not to find Hell Gate the terror that the early Dutch navigators found it, and yet I must confess this loss is in great measure made up in its ineffaceable beauty." Maybe in his day. In the days of the Dutch and before, the flatlands were vast, though the vastness could be taken in a single fill of the eye, across the width of the island to a long ridge of hills, the north-south spine of Manhattan island.

Despite its outdatedness, my 1909 map is still a living document. The terrain up here—the flatland and the ridges that encompass it—still exists, its elevations and hills still detectable, physically unchanged but perhaps psychically diminished, invisible in the long view, lined as it is with straight streets and avenues and filled with the city. There is something about grid plans that as they square off regular plats of surface, they also seem to psychically level that surface, as though a third, flat dimension is to be included. The whole of the flats near Hell Gate Bay cannot be taken in panorama, but one can track through it and discern its gradations and edges, even in some places its watery holes. What evidence of it remains? Plenty, though pretty much all of it hidden and circumstantial. At least one thin blue rivulet shown on my 1909 map still flows noisily above ground for a short distance in Central Park, and there are various pools, and hills and rocks. I walk west, intending to collect some trace evidence and scout contours, to find again the living stream that descended from the hills of the park and which I suspect emptied ultimately into Hell Gate Bay.

The flatness of the bogs that saturated this area is now the flatness of asphalt and concrete. On hot humid days it feels as though the miasma still bubbles up to penetrate the skin. Old warehouses, storehouses, lumber yards, and various low-rises still exist, and those not being demolished are being converted. Re-use extends itself throughout the neighborhood: firehouses to modern townhouses, warehouses to parking garages or designer supermarkets; tenements updated, gentrified, the whole of this place—what landscape theorist Alan Berger calls "drosscape"—an ode to industrial chic, a new pastoral. On 90th Street, the Weprin & Glass Building now houses an Avis Rent a Car. A building next door, its name obliterated, is a parking garage. The façade of the old St Joseph's Chapel belonging to the orphanage that used to occupy this block was left intact when the chapel was converted to a parking garage and then to an apartment building.

I draw my own maps as a guide to my own clambering, as though to draw them is to incorporate the local landscape into a single appreciable unit, mere inked lines on printed street maps, arrows to denote the length and direction of downward slopes, thicker lines to denote their steepness. The flats are really a wide sink, bounded by ridges, one that extends across town in the upper 90s, and the other that forms the north-south spine of Manhattan on the west side, up to about 150th Street, where the spine meets the Harlem River in a series of bluffs and cliffs. Looking north from 90th Street and Third Avenue, one can see the gradual sloping into flatness, a flatness so long and straight that when the avenue was first laid out and before any appreciable real estate development took hold, it was something of a racetrack for opportunistic young men who raced along on horseback. Walking west up 96th Street, I make cursory surveys. The neighborhood here is called Carnegie Hill, for Andrew Carnegie, the industrialist and builder of local libraries. The hill itself steepens as you move west and peaks more or less at about Park Avenue and 93rd Street. From this point, the streets and the avenue slope downward. From 96th and Third, looking east, a sharp decline to the river; at Lexington and 103rd, a sudden descent northward, the subway entrance cutting into the slope. At Park and 97th Street, Metro North trains eject from the tunnel that begins in the caverns of Grand Central Terminal at 42nd Street and emerge onto an elevated structure over Park Avenue. Stand on Park Avenue in a little park in the avenue's median, and the panorama opens up east and north into the Bronx, past the Harlem River occluded from view.

The ridge up and down the west side—Manhattan's backbone, its water-shed, marking the divide between water running west and water running east—runs roughly along the old Bloomingdale Road, which is more or less today's Broadway. All the water west flows into the Hudson, all the water east (which is most of it) flows into the meadows and bogs before emptying into the East and Harlem Rivers. In the northeast corner of Central Park is a pond called Harlem Meer. I believe this and the thin stream that feeds it are holdovers from the island's early days. I once joined a tour group. Our guide, David Karabell, was a volunteer for the Central Park Conservancy and a lawyer by profession. He was erudite, knowledgeable of the region's history and ecology. He was droll. Standing by the Harlem Meer (Dutch: "lake"), he explained some oddities. The Meer on this torpid day (August 10) was covered with a layer of green duckweed, expansive and still. Despite it appearing as a carpet, it is a food source to the ducks of the pond, who on this day did not partake, perhaps, David said, because they were not at the moment hungry. The Meer is surrounded by plane trees, planted by Robert Moses, and cypresses, which thrive near the water. David told a story to one of the kids in the group about once seeing a hawk scoop up a mouse, the mouse screaming wildly as the hawk flew away. If we see something like that today, David told the boy, you'll have something to remember. He threw out a question to us: there are more bird species in Central Park now than there were a hundred and more years ago. "Anyone know why?" A woman, deft at lateral thinking, spoke up: "Because they have nowhere else to go." Correct. There are fewer green spaces today, so the birds all collect here, their city of trees. The Meer, shallow and wide, is stocked with fish. Fishermen cast a line, catch and then throw back what they've caught. Fish caught here are without exception too small, too bony, to be of any use, not to mention it is illegal to remove them from the Meer. Catch and release. You catch a fish, incorporate the act into memory, and toss it back into the water.

The park, famous for looking natural while being artificial, really does looks natural up here, the most primeval part of the park, a couple of hundred feet above sea level, hilly, densely wooded, and off the regular paths, impossible to pass through. It cannot all be the product of artificial landscaping, too many hills and huge rocks jutting from the earth. *All the rocks.* Our guide David told us a mnemonic to keep everything straight: "Manhattan is gneiss, but the Bronx is schist." Clever, but the joke fell dead. Perhaps most of the group was from the Bronx. The creek we walked along, narrow and fast, that empties into the Meer, runs northeast through a ravine, another Victorian fantasyland of pools and ravines, grottos, niches, stone-arch bridges built without mortar, narrow dirt paths along the banks, and hewed wood rails. The creek runs into and underneath a swimming pool, Lasker Pool, into the Meer, and then disappears underground. This, I believe, is the creek I am looking for, the one that continues its course underground all the way to Hell Gate Bay.

"Naturalistic/composed" was David's term for this enclave of nature. Nature, he said, is a fabulous disarray: emphasis on disarray—nature, not as birdsong and lovely greenery, but as a howling wilderness. But, as he explained, it is not so natural here: the paths we trod are carefully planned and wrought. Underneath are sixty-two miles of pipe. The stream, its cascades and falls, all are composed; the stone bridges and niches, composed; the wooden knotty rails of the footbridges, composed. The stream, called the Loch by the Central Park officials, was at one time called Montanye's Rivulet, a name prominent in these parts, a Huguenot settlement of families that settled here primarily to farm tobacco. The Dutch were famous for allowing all sorts of foreigners and religious persuasions into their colony. They are said to have welcomed everybody, David went on, but in truth they didn't care. One supposes religious differences don't mean much in a commercial zone—it's easy to tolerate what isn't important.

The stream, murmuring and noisy, was not itself; it was reinvented by the park architects. David noticed I had been all along writing in my notebook. "I see you're taking copious notes, he said." "Question," I said: "Does this stream empty into the East River?"

"Indirectly," he answered.

The stream runs into the bogs that empty into the river. I once saw a turtle in the creek. A lone fisherman stood at the edge of the stream. He mentioned to me that turtles are common. So are guppies. "Bass, too," he said, "legal up to one pound . . . but I'm trying for catfish."

"Catfish?"

"This is all very unnatural here."

CHAPTER 3

Archipelago

Archipelagus

Block's figurative map depicts a curious arrangement of islands in the *Helle-gat*. The group is identified as the "Archipelagus," a set of identically sized and small circular islands, arranged in double-file just off the mainland. Mapmakers lacked information to identify all these islands in their true position and their actual shape and size. And though this arrangement is stylized and provisional, the picture is not far wrong, serving in the meantime to give mariners a picture of the dangers they might face. No experienced mariner would mistake the neat lineup for actuality. But the Archipelagus appears not to be the collection of islands we are most familiar with in Hell Gate, but instead to be those beyond a thin peninsula reaching south from the mainland, what is now called Throgs Neck. So one might assume these islands are those just off the shoreline of Westchester and southwestern Connecticut, including City Island and Hart Island, the Pelham islands, Mansuring (off Rye, New York), David's Island, and several small islands and rocks that loom at harbor and river mouths, as wells as several islands that no longer exist, having long since been joined to the mainland—Hunter's Island and Twin Islands, among them.

Not that Block ignored the Hell Gate islands: his map throws some shapes into the pit of water between the Bronx and Long Island, below the Archipelagus, but it was years later, in 1639, that the so-called Manatus map ("Manhattan, located on the North River") depicted these islands accurately in size and shape and located them precisely in the places we know them to be. The largest of them:

Tenkenas: The "Wild Lands"

Crossing the footbridge at 103rd street from Manhattan onto Ward's Island, you get the sense of the wild land implicit in the name *Tenkenas*. You get a sense of crossing into a different place, but it is not for the water underneath, and not for the movement from city to island, and not for the mystique of bridge transits. It is more the sudden death of traffic noise. On the Manhattan side, the FDR is a continuous flow of cars and trucks whose din only moments ago was enough to split your head. But as you ascend the arch of the bridge's roadbed, the din diminishes until after the crest of the arch, and on your descent the din is finally gone. Look back and see a silent movie of traffic.

Once, there were three islands out here in the middle of Hell Gate, and though each had several names in the past, we can call them by their latest: Ward's, Randall's, and Sunken Meadow—Ward's, the largest of the three, at the northern edge of Hell Gate Basin; Randall's, less than half the size and north of Ward's, and once separated by a sluice known as Little Hell Gate; and Sunken Meadow a small geological afterthought of sand east of Randall's. In the 1930s, when these islands were discovered by Robert Moses, he used them as anchorages for the Triborough Bridge and sought to develop them into parks and athletic fields. He began filling in the watery gaps between them, first attaching Sunken Meadow to Ward's. By the 1960s, incremental creeping into Little Hell Gate was completed, and Ward's and Randall's became one. Moses knitted these islands together, as he wished to do to all of New York. He kept his main office on Randall's Island, close to the Triborough. He wielded power: everyone who visited him here, including the politicians whom he worked for, had to pay the bridge toll.

Ward's Island, two hundred and twenty acres of rolling hills, meadows, and bogs of woods at the edges, was called *Tenkenas* by its Lenape inhabitants, a word usually translated as "wild lands." Later name shifts begat Barents, Buchanan's, Great Barn, and now Ward's, the name that stuck, after two brothers whose attempt to develop the island in the early 1800s was only the first to meet with failure.

The narrow channel that separates Manhattan and Ward's Island is either a section of the East River or the Harlem; opinions vary, owing one supposes to the inexactness of boundaries on water. The channel is narrow, generally placid, a route for small craft, the Circle Line, NYPD boats, the occasional crew team. The footbridge is a lift span, thin and tall, its middle section raised by hoisting itself elevator-like by chains between the two towers that house the chains. The lift was created for ships too tall to pass the fifty-foot clearance. But nothing that tall even attempts the passage anymore.

The shapes on Ward's Island differ from Manhattan's rectangles: the land here undulates, and pathways curve. Moses championed the creation of athletic fields and built Downing Stadium, which would host track and field meets, as well as Olympic tryouts. The stadium and fields were used for a few decades but fell into neglect or became outdated. Only a few years ago the island was retreating to raw space, unkempt and neglected: water fountains with rusted basins, erupted and disintegrating asphalt walkways, fast-growing weeds everywhere. Later came fields covered with wood chips, and then grass, an uptick on the timeline of a history of vacillation between a state of improvement and letting it all go to hell. Lately, progress has peaked (again) in the form of sodded baseball and soccer fields. Signage points the way and enlivens the place with bits of history. You'll find clean restrooms, gardens, trimmed grass, and a mix of public and private funding, not to mention space, light, air, the dirt turned over and aerated to allow young plantings to peek through—all this plus the tumult of Hell Gate waters in front of where you stand, as calming as a city fountain. To those who find beauty in dereliction, you are several years too late. Perhaps the vacillation that has run through the island's history can be explained: parks are not wild lands, but close enough that if not maintained fervently they will fall back easily to their feral state. They are that close, and there is not always enough money. It was always the character of this place to have no single character, no single vision, but rather to be a shifting of visions and energies of different groups at different times: a manor, a working mill, a dumping ground for the wayward and insane, a potter's field . . . to what it is today, a multi-use facility containing halfway houses, ballfields, recreational facilities, docks for DPA ships, FDNY training, one home for as many disparate occupancies as will fit.

It is a curious name though: Tenkenas, "wild lands." Why here? When the entire region in the time of the Lenape was wild, why would this place be called "wild lands"? Of course, that is but one of several possible translations:

"forest" and "bushy land" have also been suggested. Ruttenber proposes "small island," perhaps in comparison with Manhattan and Long Island. George Tooker suggests "uninhabited place," a place apart from the regions that saw settlement, movement, activity—a "commons" of a sort, a place with no focus, no center to its story. But the Dutch saw possibilities, or at least one governor did—for himself. Wouter van Twiller, Director-General of New Netherland from 1633 to 1638, thought Tenkenas to be a suitable place to raise cattle, the interior highlands being rich and arable, and so sought to make the island his personal ranch, buying it from a Lenape chief named Sessys ("viper"). "The most beautiful spot on earth," was Van Twiller's assessment, but he never lived here, content to use the land as an investment.

John Flavel Mines, as he sat at his summer house on the East River, thought Ward's Island to be the most picturesque of any of the Hell Gate landscapes. So did many others who came and went. Over the centuries, the islands changed owners many times, and with each change came a change of name. A Swede named Barents (or Barendt) bought what would become Ward's Island in the 1700s, and thus it took his name. A shuffling of ownership and identities ensued. Great Barn Island might have been a printer's error for Barents. (Such accidents in toponymy are common and easy to understand; I have more than once typed Heel Gate.) Buchanan's was another. The smaller island to the north became Montresor's, named after the British engineer and military officer John Montresor, who bought and used the island as a country manor for himself and his family, although his duties of war and surveying kept him away most of the time. In 1784, the Ward brothers Jasper and Bartholomew bought the larger island and began to citify it. They opened a cotton mill, constructed a footbridge to connect the island to Manhattan, and built houses for themselves on the perimeter of the island overlooking Hell Gate. But the cotton mill failed after the War of 1812, and a storm in 1821 destroyed the bridge, ending in one short stroke the Wards' hopes for a city island.

Little Hell Gate

Continuing my search for ruins and isolation by way of distance, I walked up the west side of the island, heading to a cove called Little Hell Gate, a small nook of water indented into the side of the modern island, a vestige of the sluice that separated Ward's and Randall's Islands. It was low tide in the channel on this visit, seawalls and rip-rap dry but water-stained, the shore front exposed. Small waves broke several yards offshore in the shallow water just beyond the flats. I played by the shore front, snapping pictures of rocks and rip-rap, the maw of outflow pipes, the alluvial imprints in the sand. Scrambling across the rip-rap, I fell upward, my feet quickly and awkwardly looking for solid footing, which I managed to find, without spraining an ankle or catching a foot in a crevice. Along the dirt walkway, gardens, cultivation: shade trees, flowers—achillea, lavender, daisies, something from the onion family, big bulbous spears sitting atop tall spindly stalks—all meant to beautify a nondescript asphalt path.

The path bends to the east with the shoreline. In its day, Little Hell Gate was a wide channel, navigable by small craft and fully susceptible to the currents of Hell Gate, rendering them even more perplexing than they are today. All that's left is its western mouth, now a cove about two hundred feet wide or so at its opening. Tree limbs between the path and the shorefront droop almost to the water; one has rotted and cracked, fallen not quite off its trunk but enough so that its top sits in the shallow water. Little Hell Gate is a good place to study the ancient islands, the cove a reminder, or a leftover, of the place that once was. Isolation often provokes unease in the city, but not here. Strangers pass by, but they have no ill intention toward you, no intention at all but to move on. So quiet is the place that sudden eruptions of noise are startling: a whirring coming from around a bend and up the hill—a cyclist descends and speeds by. A sudden flurry from the brush: a squirrel pops out to sit on its haunches and beg—but sorry, friend, I've got nothing for you: no nuts, no spare change. His presence reminds me that some creatures really are of the city, no longer wild but conditioned to human habits and with humanlike expectations.

A wooden footbridge supported by twin steel arches and bedded with wooden planks traverses the cove several yards in from its mouth. The cove begins to funnel here into a narrow inlet that circles alongside the marsh, and an even narrower one that enters and describes a sinuous s-curve into its interior. The incoming tide wells these inlets; the outgoing tide nearly drains them. Signs placed in panels along the bridge describe a chain of being in local life: blue crabs (bottom-dwelling predators), Atlantic ribbed mussels, grass shrimp and sand shrimp . . . two types of killifish, chubs and minnows that move through the cordgrass (which can grow to seven feet), searching for food such as phytoplankton, mosquito larvae, and small crustaceans . . . the common mummichog, "a native American word that means 'going in crowds,' a name that accurately describes the schooling behavior of all killifish" (as well as the human population of the city of New York) . . . the Atlantic silverside, which, unlike killifish, is sensitive to changes in its environment and feeds on zooplankton, shrimp, worms, algae, and in turn becomes prey for bluefish, striped bass, egrets, cormorants, terns.

Contemporary fishermen speak of the same species that their counterparts knew centuries ago: blue fish, flounder, snapper, porgies, and eels. John Flavel Mines writes of the fish that inhabited these waters a hundred years ago, pretty much the same species we see today: tomcods and eels, striped bass of "mammoth size," lobster, flounder. Mysteries of language and translation: Mines cites a list of creatures Adriaen van der Donck included in his New Netherland anatomy: "snook, forrels, palings, dunns, and scolls," and claims he has no idea what a "snook" is. It is a tropical fish, and whether the Dutch actually found it here is questionable. Paling is eel (Dutch: *Gerookte paling*, a Dutch delicacy, is smoked eel). As with the naming of their rivers, the Dutch had their naming systems with fish. From Van der Donck:

> First in the season they caught many shad which they named *Elft*, (eleventh.). Later they caught the striped bass which they named *Twalft*, (twelfth.) Later still they caught the drums, which they named *Dertienen*, (thirteenth.) For those fish succeeded each other their seasons and the same are still known by the names which thus derived.

There exists an urban legend about lobsters that continued for centuries. The Dutch tried for lobster in New Amsterdam waters, found none, and decided to import them from New England. On its way through the Gate, one of their boats hit a rock and sank, freeing the lobsters to escape by drifting and falling with the currents to new homes on the floors of New York waters. Oysters once thrived in New York waters, in Upper New York Bay and Jamaica Bay, especially—Pearl Street, along the original shoreline of Manhattan, is named for the oysters once found there—but also near Hell Gate and further on in the East River to the northeast. They were plentiful: in the nineteenth century, much of the world's supply came from New York harbor. And their plenty also made them cheap, and easily harvested: raking them for food or sale was a small-time family occupation. What killed them of course was overharvesting and pollution. But now there are groups (the Billion Oyster Project, most notably) intent on reviving them, using spent shells as seed beds, often donated by local restaurants—oysters thrive best when bedded in the calcified remains of their own ancestors, and as well among the hard, manmade substrates like the limestone or concrete used to make bulwarks or chunks deposited as rip-rap, as at Little Hell Gate.

It is impossible to snap a picture of the marsh and its footbridge without extraneous matter of the city closing in at the edges. Unless you stand tall on a ledge and aim down, your view will include the Triborough Bridge viaduct or Icahn Stadium, Manhattan State Hospital or Manhattan Island's east side. The photographers for the Randall's Island Park Alliance website have deftly solved this problem by cropping out tops and bottoms, leaving long and sweeping horizontals of marsh. Juxtaposition of city and primal can't otherwise be avoided, or maybe that's the real theme. In the shadows of the viaducts, concrete barriers are painted with colorful silhouettes of birds: sanctioned graffiti. Things of the city are prominent enough to make the place look like a fabricated scene, which in fact it is, a display: stock plantings of cord grasses set in a small area where they might thrive, and evidently do. The whole of this place is something of a demonstration, an area set apart and seeded with specimens to become a working engine of self-generation, a rest area for passing birds, a stationary ark for plants, crawlers, and fliers. A return to origins that took planning and action, not neglect: the expunging of urban ruin and garbage. The logical consequence of which is the return of a small sector to something like a model of the primal Tenkenas in action, primal being its intended future. The whole, including the snaking inlet, reminds me of a landscape art project. The future will require maintenance, a constant human intervention to keep up appearances, unless like most works of landscape art it is allowed to degenerate into its urban surroundings.

The wake of a boat that had passed in the channel some minutes before now arrives: a small, slow-moving tsunami, a single wave the width of the creek mouth and now entering the channel under the footbridge, invading unstoppably all the way through to the gyres of the inlet. Not far behind, another wave, and then a third. The tide is turning inward. The incoming waves advance tsunami-like in speed, spacing, and precision, if not in height and danger. The waves pass under the footbridge and into the inlet, and as they do the ends of each crest buck up against the retaining walls and then rebound to the other side, which being so near send a rebound back to the first. What were waves so distinct and precise now lose their singularity and devolve into a churn of water. The churning only compounds and aggravates itself, and ends in noise and violence before settling again into calm. Here in this model universe is another demonstration of what used to be the chaos of Little Hell Gate, and the larger one outside.

CHAPTER 4

Hell Gate Circle

A Winter Walk

Someone at the Department of Transportation has a sense of humor: a road looping through the interior of Ward's Island is named Hell Gate Circle. If places should come with a geometric motif attached, then the circle should be Hell Gate's: "hell" of the public imagination, the circle being its symbol, at least since Dante constructed the place as a set of concentric rings. So far, I had stuck near to the island's perimeter on my walks, but now my attention was turning inland. I poked around the anchorage at the base of the Hell Gate Arch Bridge. Here I came upon a small encampment, consisting of a small fire pit, long extinguished, an old sleeping bag, unidentifiable pieces of clothing, fast-food wrappings, colors and print bleared from past rains: the insatiable longing for aloneness and autonomy. Ramshackle, a cheap motel, which made it all the more desperate. Weeds flattened from sleeping bodies... illegible graffiti fading on the stone anchorage of the bridge: BILLY BOY, it looks like—unsure of the rest, and given the flamboyance of the penmanship not even sure of that. Someone had marked this place, maybe one of its transient tenants. Many travelers have no doubt been through here, taking it as theirs for the time spent. I stuck around a while, thinking someone might come back. He might be at this moment crouching in the bushes thither, spying, trying to out-game me, not waiting to strike, but rather for me to leave. And if we were to make contact, what was I to do? Ask him questions? "What is it like, sir, to live at the base of the Hell Gate Arch Bridge? Does the rumble of the trains lull you to sleep at night, or keep you awake? Does the darkness make you feel safe? Or does it embolden potential predators?"

The winter ground is still sodden from a recent rain, and all that lingering duck or goose shit—thankfully, I had the presence of mind this morning to put on good hiking boots. The island is in low dress, a good day to seek out more ruins and relics, more landscape, the weather a guarantee that most citizens will stay away, leaving things undisturbed. Winter, like night, offers a different perspective, a new feel to the place: less active, barer, sparser, in part because of the bareness of the trees and hardness of the ground. In part, too, because of a different population. No families of summer, no athletes, not even soccer players or runners today (a weekday). Along Hell Gate Circle, a pleasant drive around the inside perimeter, are various shelters and hospitals, the contemporary replacements for the massive asylums and hospitals that once occupied these grounds. Despite the sun, the place feels forlorn, and the isolation conferred by distance from the city is unsettling. I have the typical New Yorker's unease in wide-open spaces: too much space for bad things to happen.

Did the namer of the street have Dante in mind, or rather the quaint names given to streets in suburban subdivisions? Walking along the island's southern and eastern rims and into the interior, I see only a few people, and after a

time I notice that these few are all men. Even the Parks Department person-
nel are all men, patrolling in their vans and carts, gathering the dead leaves
that have drifted up against the fences separating the soccer fields. But the
others, too, the walkers, whether alone or in pairs, are all men, footloose wanderers treading defined paths, hands pocketed in heavy coats. Hats pulled far
down make it easy to avert one's eyes. They emerge from behind tall hedges or
viaduct piers and then disappear down a path, around a bend. They walk with
purpose, whatever that purpose may be. One man walks, and then abruptly
breaks into a sprint. The unknowableness of purpose: it took me a moment to
realize he was running for exercise, not to make tracks. Other men material-
ize before me. A fellow comes to a boulder set in the ground, positions his
foot on the boulder to brace himself, and tilts his head upward to get his tan
from a gauzy sun. He freezes, and remains so for so long that I begin to think
I had hallucinated his arrival moments before, that he has always been here.
A raft of ducks sits still above the Hog Back just offshore, the shape of their
mass changing slowly with the movement of the water. Various shapes coming and forming into something else, liquids slowing down, becoming solid:
the weather, cold and dry but a strong wind. A man in a long greatcoat and
sneakers passes by and says to me, "It'll kill you out here," though what I hear
is, "They'll kill you out here." But, no: it was a friendly comment—the wind,
he meant, not the company. Far ahead, I see a Parks man pull up in a van at the
Island Café, closed today, and, bless him, unlock the door on the one public
bathroom I know of out here.

A Melancholy Rag

Perhaps *Tenkenas* is a suitable name: "wild lands," "uninhabited place," meaning uninhabitable, a no-man's-land. Which means everyone's. Following the
Ward brothers' attempt to civilize their island came a period of abandonment. Abandonment encourages found use, transitory claimants, not so legal
proprietorships. A topography of hills and coves encourages hiding: disparate
and stealthy parties seize the opportunity to hide things, store things, dump
things, from cattle to stolen goods, not to mention, later, immigrants, drunks,
and the insane, acres of free space to accommodate mass burial. An island of
possibility.

For thieves, the island and the surrounding waters were inviting, water in a waterborne city yet another source of plunder. So it was natural that some of their more plucky numbers would extend their activities to rivers and docks. River pirates prowled the waterfront, climbing onto ships at dockside, or else rowing out into the dark harbor to pester ships at anchor waiting on a change of tide. Occasionally, the thieves worked alone: one iconoclast named Slipsey Ward tried to take a schooner single-handed, and was busted easily. For the most part, though, they worked concertedly in gangs, and these gangs ran the gamut, from the losers who pilfered ship tackle and mostly useless articles for sale at clandestine outlets, to the violent. These were not your Hollywood swashbucklers but more the petty thief and goofy marauder. Hell Gate was itself a place for lying-in-wait. Thieves in the night, but daybreak was also a special time. The best-known gang to work the Gate were the Daybreak Boys, named for their habit of striking just before dawn, and also for their age—almost to a man they were boys in their teens. Being young and energetic, they were naturally athletic and could move with catlike grace and silence. But style and finesse were not their strong suit; brute plunder was, and should anyone get in the way, murder was one way out. But they knew the waters and the habits of sailors, who slept at night.

To say the Daybreak boys were organized might be an overstatement: one does not imagine military control, but rather a loose and opportunistic confederation. Nevertheless, two in particular emerged as captains of a sort: William Saul and Nicholas Howlett. One night in August 1852, after a convivial evening of drink, talk, and tenpins, Saul and some friends met up with Howlett outside a saloon near the docks. Saul and Howlett, and a third, a drunk named Johnson, went for a joyride in Howlett's boat, aiming to see what was there for the taking among the many schooners berthed along the wharves. Saul borrowed Howlett's pistol for protection. Saul and Howlett—poor Johnson too stupid to do anything but lay drunk in the boat—climbed aboard a schooner, saw that the watchman was awake, and exited. They rowed along, climbed onto a brig, and the watchman there too was awake. They climbed a third, a schooner called the Thomas Watson, and seeing the watchman was asleep, calmly stepped over him to grab a watch and a pair of pants, presumably the watchman's. The watchman, a fellow named Charles Baxter, awoke, and a brief altercation followed, ending when Saul fired a shot in the man's direction, intending, as thieves tend to say, to scare him, but which scored a hit, killing Baxter. Saul and Howlett returned to their boat and rowed to shore. Someone on shore had heard the shot. The thieves were caught. What followed was the kind of criminal comedy so often repeated in police interrogations. Cool and cocky, Saul exclaimed to his jailers, "Oh, you can never convict us, and mum is the word." They were convicted. Only when Johnson was also convicted did Saul and Howlett reveal a momentary flash of goodness in their otherwise deteriorated souls: they told the full story, explaining that Johnson had nothing to do with the murder. Saul and Howlett were hanged in the yard at the Tombs in January, 1853. Saul was twenty-one, and Howlett twenty. River thievery did not abate after this, but this particular case brought it to public attention.

As might be expected in a place where different groups established them-selves, thieves and inmates would accidentally cross paths and stumble into each other's private domain, often with a bad result. Not much policing took place on the rivers, and even less on Ward's Island. A newspaper article tells of a run-in between river thieves—bones and bed-ticking being their plunder, and one James Ritchie, an asylum inmate, a "harmless imbecile":

> . . . herding cows near the old house. A heifer got frightened and began romping and jumping around. Ritchie ran after the unruly beast toward the shore and the pile of bones. When pretty near the latter point he saw three men, who had evidently come to rob the pile, and who had a small boat drawn up on the shore nearby. Just as Ritchie caught sight of them, one of them, who apparently thought the lunatic was an official running to intercept his party, threw up his hand, a flash followed, and Ritchie fell to the ground with a bullet-hole in his head.

A journalist described the transients here as a "floating population," an apt metaphor for Hell Gate, the place of transit with its stories of coming and going. Once the city took over the island in the 1840s, after the Ward brothers had packed it in, the island became home to the outcasts and the sick, the "home to the friendless," like cigar-shaped Blackwell's to the south, except here was more room to lose oneself—about two hundred and twenty acres. The city purchased the island outright in 1851, and for the next several decades, New York City and New York State erected numerous hospitals, almshouses, and asylums: the Emigrants Hospital, for destitute immigrants; the Lunatic Asylum, later replaced with a newer and larger Lunatic Asylum; the Inebriates Asylum (for opium-addicted Civil War vets, opened in 1868 and closed a few years later because it was found that "forcible detention" was not a cure for addiction or alcoholism); an "Idiot Asylum"; nurseries for children on Randall's Island; and a House of Refuge for Juvenile Delinquents. Later still came Manhattan State Hospital for the Insane. Some were handsome facilities, some built according to the Kirkbride Plan, in which a core building was appended with a series of wings, emphasizing openness and airiness, something like a college campus.

A look at the menu showed a wholesome diet for the inmates of the Ward's Island houses: boiled or roasted meats, potatoes, vegetables every day, soup, bread, coffee, milk, tea, water. Surrounding the buildings were groves of trees, reservoirs, even a sluice of water from Little Hell Gate in which inmates could bathe. Institutional literature made it all sound like resort life—everything looks better on paper. But good looks were on the outside only. Facilities were crowded, in fact overcrowded; the insane were often mixed in with the drunks; attendants were few, and fewer were trained; nights were punctuated with howling and profanity. Inmates beat up other inmates. When overcrowding became unbearable, populations were shifted from building to building. All of the facilities built in the nineteenth century were eventually closed and demolished, but Manhattan State Hospital lived on in a different form. It exists today, a large yellowish facility, imposing institutional architecture, now called the Kirby Forensic Psychiatric Center, a house for the criminally insane with a name that smooths over the reality.

On many occasions while I am out here, a rag composition comes to mind, and I let it play itself out in my head: the "Magnetic Rag," by Scott Joplin, which some musicologists consider his most melancholic, as its tempo might suggest: *allegretto ma non troppo*—almost happy but not too much, ghost music from a hidden room, not just whistling a happy tune. A certain mood is elicited. This not only because of the melancholic season and place, but that this particular rag was one of Joplin's last, in fact the last to be published in his lifetime, and one of the last he finished before losing his mind, and then his life, to syphilis. Joplin spent his last living days on Ward's Island, at Manhattan State.

I come to the Charles H. Gay Center, a small, unimposing, red-brick building, to ask of its origins: Was this Manhattan State before the big one was
built? I knock on the door's glass panel, and the men inside, perhaps thinking I am looking for work, motion through the glass to another door across
the hall. At the Mabon Building, not far away, I ask my question: "Was this
Manhattan State before the big one was built?" An attendant suggests that
I "Google it." My question contains a second question that I do not care to
voice: Was this where Scott Joplin spent his last days? Another attendant
comes forward and tells me the building was built around 1918. That was the
year after Joplin died.

Scott Joplin (1868–1917) was the author of rags, marches, and waltzes, celebrated in his lifetime, and then more or less forgotten, until the 1970s when
Joshua Rifkin recorded several pieces for the Nonesuch record label. Joplin
did not invent ragtime, but he was regarded as its prime creative spirit. The
path that brought him to Ward's Island was long and circuitous. He was born
in Texarkana, on the border of Texas and Arkansas. He had an early affinity for
music, playing guitar and bugle, and became good enough on piano to warrant
lessons from a German music teacher, who introduced him to classical music.
Joplin also had an affinity for wandering, leaving Texarkana when only four-
teen to play popular piano music, mostly in the sporting houses of red-light
districts in St. Louis and Sedalia, Missouri. His wandering was not so much
that of a restless spirit but because it was a musician's life to follow the money.
He played popular songs and an innovative music called ragtime. Ragtime was
a new form: white harmonies on top of black polyrhythms, new rhythms and
themes that would (later) be absorbed by the likes of Debussy and Stravinsky
in their own quests to discover new forms. In 1899, the year Maple Leaf Rag
was published, Joplin handed a coin to a friend with that date: "Keep this," he
said, "the Maple Leaf Rag will make me King of Ragtime." It did.

Joplin was a serious student, reserved, sober, and his reserve and talent
magnetic. He was ambitious. He envisioned operas, perhaps symphonies. He
wrote an opera, *A Guest of Honor*, which was performed once in St. Louis.
The score has since been lost. While composing and publishing numerous
rags in the 1900s, Joplin still imagined operas and complex scores. He composed waltzes, slow drags, and a lovely serenade with a tango rhythm, perhaps suggestive of what he sought: "Solace," what he described as "A Mexican

Serenade." He began another opera, ambitious and complex, *Treemonisha*, *Opera in Three Acts*, the story of a slave girl. He tried to settle down, to purge himself of the wandering life. From St. Louis, he moved to Chicago, and thence to New York, settling into a house on west 47th Street, near the music centers of the city. Later, he went to Harlem.

Two things began to bear down on him: one, mounting *Treemonisha*; two, syphilis. *Treemonisha* was his obsession: three acts, twenty-seven set pieces, each numbered separately in the score, a score for eleven voices with piano accompaniment. Its subject was being a black girl in America and involved slavery, voodoo, and a quest for freedom. The idea was too much for investors. He could not find a publisher for the score and paid for publication out of his own pocket. Nevertheless, he continued to look for investors, and in 1915 he mounted a performance, really a rehearsal without all the sets and costumes, in order to attract investors. It did not go well: his mostly black audience was not ready for reminders of recent history.

Joplin's mind was slowly fragmenting. He began work but did not finish it. He played a Maple Leaf Rag for a piano roll . . . but within months his abilities descended to a point that the tune that had made him famous was barely recognizable. He was brought to Manhattan State, his sanity slowly ebbing, to live out his last instance of hell. When it was over, he was buried in St. Michael's Cemetery, Astoria, on the other side of Hell Gate.

Transit

Hell Gate presents puzzles of history, events with a believe-it-or-not quality, more Ripley than Dante, a sideshow, a cabinet of curiosities. Of the odd stories, the Corpse Box is the oddest, and not entirely believable even in the straightest telling of its weird facts. It is a conflation of two Hell Gate legends: dead bodies found floating in the river ("floaters"), and the treasure ship *Hussar*, which sank at Hell Gate in 1780, supposedly laden with gold. "Tide brings in gruesome corpse-box with its weird mystery," reads a headline of a newspaper article in the *Pittsburgh Press*, of all places (April 26, 1934), "the corpse-box of Hell Gate floated by . . ."

On a hot summer day, June 1, 1859, a boat sets out for Port Morris in the Bronx to search for a treasure chest of gold supposedly lost in the accidental sinking of the old British warship, *HMS Hussar*. The captain of this boat was a fisherman named Schmidt. Accompanying him were Mrs. Schmidt, a man named Ramsay, and a number of others whose names have been lost. They intended to recover this treasure by means of hook, grappling lines, and assorted other instruments improvised to make easier the recovery of a chest of gold. After a couple of hours, they realized their tools would not work. They found no treasure. Discouraged, Mrs. Schmidt pulled herself off the search, her attention drifting. In the distance she noticed a log floating in the current toward the boat. She called out to her husband. As the log neared the boat it became obvious it was not a log, but a wooden box. Treasure still in the back of their minds—they imagined a box of gold, and if not gold, then perhaps the box itself could be sawed into planks and sold. Hauling it aboard with great difficulty, they noticed an encrusted lock sealing lid to box. Opening the box was a matter of breaking the lock, which a single blow accomplished. The box did not contain gold, but human bodies. Stunned and more than a little frightened, the party called the authorities. The coroner ascertained the remains of seven bodies: three men (two whites, one black—a fact that becomes important to the legend that grew around this story), two women, a child, and an infant. Days later, the authorities, led by Mayor Tiermann, concluded the box had slipped off a boat transporting bodies to the potter's field on Ward's Island. However, certain facts interfered with these conclusions: for one, even paupers in potter's fields were buried in individual boxes, not several crammed into a single large box.

It was years later that a writer of boys' adventure books named Eliot O'Donnell sought to explain the mystery of the box, planning to include his solution in a book of sea stories. His theory relied on legends involving slavery and pre–Civil War true crime stories, but he had no supporting evidence. In his story, the dead in the box were all members of a family of southern planters named Garcia. One of the slaves belonging to them, a half-breed named Fernando, jealous of the family, had lured them into traveling north. In a house along the way, Fernando murdered them individually, loaded them into the single wooden box, sealed it, and sent it adrift in the ocean. Currents carried it into New York Harbor, up the East River, and through Hell Gate (the vortex of all that is evil). Meanwhile, other members of Fernando's gang had robbed and burned the train that the Garcias were expected to arrive on.

A story as blarney as Bram Stoker, as tedious as J.F. Cooper. But the central image—the East River as an avenue of death—that is real.

The playing fields and grassy knolls of Ward's Island take on a more melancholic aspect when one realizes that under them is an abode of the dead. Graves here are scattered, their provenance not always known, and details scanty. One may presume that burials have taken place since the earliest occupations of the wild lands. A small party comes across a placement of rocks and presumes they are markers for graves. Indians, some of them expect, but more likely British soldiers who occupied the island during the Revolutionary War. Indians did not mark graves, but white men did, needing, in the words of John Flavel Mines, the "protecting arms of the oak or elm."

It was around the time Mines was writing that a party of inmates and laborers were engaged in an excavation project on the island near the chaplain's house. Digging, they hit stone. Clearing away more dirt, they uncovered a granite slab under which were stone steps leading to a vault. Some of the diggers were certain the vault belonged to Captain Kidd, who was known to live in New York, but their supposition was based on the hope for buried treasure rather than evidence. On the chamber's paved floor were four wooden coffins in despicable shape. Three nearly disintegrated at the touch. The superintendent stopped his crew from flinging their contents around, disappointed as they were that they contained no treasure. A fourth coffin, of cherry and walnut, was in better shape. On its lid was a small inscription: a heart with the initials "I.R.," the year of death, 1737, and I.R.'s age, thirty-seven. The men left, covering up the vault with its contents in place. Who was I.R? An unsolved mystery. Assuming the "I" might stand for a Latin "J," then Joris Rapelje, the progenitor of the illustrious Walloon family whose name is left to us as Rapalye, would have made a good candidate but for the fact that he died about 1662. John Randel (or Randall), for whom Randall's Island is named, would have been another had he not come along after the death of "I.R." The writer of the article from which I make these notes closes with a rhetorical question: "Does not his grave conceal the clue to the history of Ward's Island?" I'll venture an answer: no more so than any other place where life crosses into death. Multiply one grave by thousands.

The real castaways of Hell Gate are not the victims of maritime accident so much as the exiles who were brought to its islands to get clean or because no one would have them. Or, as in the case of those for whom time had eroded identity, to be given a decent if unheralded burial. In the 1850s, a section of Ward's Island became a potter's field, a graveyard for the unknown or abandoned dead, and for those whose families were too poor or without ties to a church, or were otherwise too isolated from a community for a burial in a local churchyard. Potter's fields were mass graves because the masses who qualified numbered in the thousands. Typically, they were, and still are, located outside cities or at their edge, for reasons of public health and to remove them that much further from public consciousness. Renowned public spaces often got their start as potter's fields: Washington Square was originally a potter's field; so was Bryant Park. As the living moved nearer, the ground over the fields was reshaped and rechristened. Sometimes the dead were dug up to be moved farther away. Sometime in the 1800s, an empty space at about 49th Street and Fourth Avenue became a potter's field. But it was only a few years later that plans were made to locate a railroad north along Fourth Avenue to Harlem. So the city dug up the potter's field there and removed its nameless dead out to Randall's Island. But diggers did a sloppy job: bones were left uncovered and scattered. Dogs sniffing about ran off with bones clutched in their teeth. Boys played games of kickball with hollow skulls. If one shattered, many others were available nearby. Old bones and shards of bones were collected and taken to Randall's, and the newly deceased began their arrival as well. Even that proved unsatisfactory: the effluvia of the graves wafted north and beset the children's nurseries also located on Randall's, a bit north and down summer's wind.

A new field was opened, this one on the roomier pastures of Ward's Island to the south. Exactly where is a matter of conjecture. There are no signs to advise the curious, nothing to announce that you are standing on top of a mass grave. An old map showed an area at the southwest of the island cordoned off by dashed lines. It was unlabeled, and I took that to be exactly the sort of reference one might expect of a place to be positioned but which shall remain unmentioned. Subsequent landfill and shaping put it several yards north of where the island's edge is today. On my walks across the island I sometimes brought out my maps, indulging in a curious game, pursuing new mappings on top of old, archaeology without the digging. I counted steps, staked various layouts. I made presumptions and assumptions. My information was spurious, a few snatches of writing here and there that suggested a potter's field was once here. A newspaper account from 1855 was more than a suggestion: "Rambling about Ward's Island," written at a time when burials were an ongoing activity here and therefore a subject suitable for a feature story.

The article relates a tour taken by the Rambler (there was no by-line for this article), describing along the way the circumstances of those who were interred here and the process of their burial. The Rambler was a sunny fellow, lively, chatty—tedious, in another word. He had done this sort of tour before. His excursion to Ward's follows one he made to Trinity Churchyard, where he reviewed the burial monuments and stones of the famous. Now his quest was that of the unknown. In his article, the Rambler gives some indication of direction and points out features of landscape, but the landscape has changed so much over the intervening century and a half that these coordinates can function only as clues or hints. He left New York by street car, arriving in Harlem near an establishment called the Red House, and was rowed across the river to the Ward's Island Hospital dock, on its western flank. From there he walked south to a cove cut deeply into the island's rim, and he used his location to call attention to the errors of boats: a boat trapped in an eddy and swirling. Hell Gate "through which waters roar, and break and tumble, as if veritably they were at the mouth of a bottomless pit." Charybdis again. Nevertheless, "a glorious landscape—for we suppose where the sea most prevails there especially is a landscape."

At a house by a cove, the Rambler was greeted by Mr. Webb, the "jolly guardian of the field," who would act as tour guide. This house would be the one that appears on old maps and navigational charts, the one used by mariners as a sight point in their navigations through Hell Gate. Facing the Gate, looking south, the Rambler noted that the Hog Back is to the left, Hen and Chickens in front, Mill Rock to the right. The Rambler and Mr. Webb set out, following "a cowpath from the point up to the field—a crooked right-angled path that made it a quarter of a mile away." A knight's tour, but unfortunately he gave no cardinal directions. They stopped at a site where another house once stood, something of a focus for an old man who was born on the spot and who revisited it every year on his birthday to review the old landmarks: the house, the cove, the orchards. That year the old man failed to show, and the Rambler's presumption was that he had passed, along with the house, the passing of both going unnoticed by newspapers.

A climb up a hill and they were at the gate of the potter's field, an incredible stench to greet them. The dead, explained Mr. Webb, were put into coffins. Mr. Webb explained that the dead boats carried a continuing flow of bodies from the city. Before burial, the bodies were laid in a landing house, where they were preserved on ice. This gave some time to any who might claim the dead. After a few days, those still unclaimed, which was nearly all of them, were then prepared for burial. Their coffins were plain wood boxes, but each person was given his or her own box. Coffins were laid in trenches three hundred feet long, fifteen feet deep, eighteen feet wide, laid end to end across the width of the trench wide enough to accommodate three coffins. They were stacked in tiers until the top tier was about two feet from the surface. Then they were topped with dirt, piled higher than the ground level, which would eventually subside to ground level as the bodies and wood underneath decomposed. When a trench was completely covered, the ground above was graced with young cedar trees.

Such a tour may be impossible to trace, too much being razed and too much constructed in the meantime. Nevertheless, if the potter's field still exists its location may be surmised. I compared old maps to new, mapping coordinates. The cove where the Rambler began no longer exists, but by superimposing new maps on the old it is clear that though the cove has been filled it leaves a trace of itself as the merest indent in the island's southern rim. As near as I could tell, the cove was where two paths turn away from the water and toward the interior, leading directly to a small structure that contains a snack bar in front and restrooms in the rear. I do not know what paths existed for the Rambler; there are an infinite number of knight's tours between here and the supposed site of the field. An arc of a quarter-mile will take you from the lowlands at the west to an area of hills and knolls to the northeast. I went to the northeast, and there are good reasons to suspect this is the right direction. The landscape rolls upward, a long, steep hill. I climb the hill to find its top leveled off into an athletic field, long enough to accommodate a game of football or soccer, and now being used by a group of college men playing ultimate Frisbee, a football-like game played with a Frisbee. The men dart about the field, sailing the Frisbee to teammates downfield anticipating its arrival, watching as it floats weightlessly and free in the air, waiting for it to come down to their clutch. It is within this hill, several feet under this field, that the nameless dead most likely reside, a tumulus. Nearby are other fields, knolls—an adapted landscape.

Just beyond the field, to the northeast, is the anchorage of the Hell Gate Bridge, set on a bluff overlooking the channel. It is to just such a bluff that the Rambler walked to on his leave from the potter's field: "a few rods to the shore, which here is an abrupt wood-crowned bank." The bank is still abrupt and wood crowned. From the bluff, the Rambler took notice of the ships in the channel, noting that the existence here of the potter's field gives mariners something else to dread besides the rocks and the swift water: "the sixteen thousand ghosts of newly buried men, women and children, gibbering in the night wind, or mutely gliding and noiselessly jostling each other." Night focuses energy, reveals spirits: "It is no wonder that the sailors look up with a shudder at the spot when they pass through Hell Gate at midnight." And the wind delivering fumes across the channel.

At the anchorage of the Hell Gate Bridge, present day: I see in the inter-vening months between winter and summer walks here that the BILLY BOY graffiti on the anchorage has transmuted into something like SMELLS EDGE.

CHAPTER 5

Wandering Rocks

"O, Rocks!"

(A favorite curse of Molly Bloom's.)
Ulysses, James Joyce

From the southern rim of Ward's Island, I look south across Hell Gate Basin and down the west channel of the East River between Roosevelt Island and Manhattan. The basin is nearly a mile across at this point, east from 96th Street to Pot Cove off Hallett's Point, Astoria. Whitecaps on the water in front, bluffs of Manhattan and Astoria on either side. Another common observation point, a long and encompassing view: far downriver, and straight on is the Queensborough Bridge, its gothic intricacy lost in side elevation view. Distant tugs and barges appear to be stilled in the water. I should bring my binoculars next time, the better to see all that passes.

Two sailing ships collide and founder on the shores of Great Barn (Ward's) Island in an entanglement of mast and line. Or perhaps they foundered individually and were then brought to their mutual and inglorious end by the currents. Downriver, to the east, is a steamer, smoke rising from double stacks, which will need to thread the rocks dead ahead. This scene does not lament the age of sail in order to herald that of steam, but rather tosses both into the same boil at Hell Gate: contrariness that subjects ships to whim. In the left foreground is the whitewater of the Hog Back. Far to the right, the powder house on Mill Rock. Haze of perspective: down the long center of the frame is the river that disappears somewhere between Blackwell's Island and Corlear's Hook.

The rocks, clustered or in isolation, were the lesser elements of the archipelago, but also the gravest threat, rocks being implacable and unyielding, and to wooden ships in trouble, a stark and sudden truth, reducing strong ships

to the pitiful objects depicted in Archibald Dick's print, grounded, tilted, and generally askew. Lose control in a swift current, and if lucky you might be ejected into a patch of calm water—but hit a rock, and it's all over. Rocks that jutted up ominously at low water disappeared altogether at high, by mere inches or a few feet, exacerbating the danger. Like most of the bedrock of the surrounding islands, the rocks were a mixture of schist and gneiss, angular and planar and still jagged despite the endless tides eroding their finer edges. Some rocks, such as the Hog Back off Ward's Island, are still there, hidden just below the water's surface, creating whitewater when the tide is coming in or going out, and exposed at low water, its danger mitigated by their proximity to shore and by buoys with lights and bells that clang in the wind. Time and tide, season and moon, weather and storms, all played their part complicating navigation to the point that you were pretty much on your own, and God help you should you choose the wrong moment to come through. Daniel Denton, calling on Charon, said as much in 1670.

For the dangers they presented, rocks have figured in nautical myth, always playing the role of nemesis to the heroic mariner. Circe warned Odysseus he had a choice: to attempt a pass between Scylla and Charybdis or else to try passing through the Wandering Rocks. Jason and his Argonauts sailed amidst the Clashing Rocks at the pass between the Sea of Marmara and the Black Sea. They unleashed a bird whose tailfeathers were caught between a moving rock and the stern of their ship. That the bird survived was a good sign: they chanced passage and made it through. The Irish mystic Saint Brendan the Navigator set sail across the Atlantic Ocean in his search for paradise and, in discovering the volcanic shores of Iceland, thought instead he had arrived at Hell.

The rocks at Hell Gate entered legend early on: an Algonquin legend tells of their creation as the product of a battle between two spirits. The good Tchi-Manitou and the evil Manetto battled for the hearts and minds of the people, their fight lasting generations. Manetto, losing, retreated into a cave, where he was found by a party of hunters. He escaped, but as he was too weak to continue his fight, he ran across the water, and everywhere his foot touched, the water turned to black stone. Thus came to be the Steppingstone Rocks, a small set of rocks in Long Island Sound just off Kings Point. Further out in the Sound was Execution Rock, where English soldiers tied American prisoners just below the high-water line, giving them the opportunity to watch and think for a couple of hours about the inevitable.

American merchantmen on the "short sea"—the coastal waterway up and down the Eastern Seaboard—had a choice when entering New York harbor, through the Narrows, the mile-wide gap between Brooklyn and Staten Island, or through the "back door" of the East River and Hell Gate, with its rocks and turns. Despite its dangers, the Dutch saw the East River as a good commercial route. Adriaen van der Donck, advertising the colony at New Amsterdam, noted its benefits for passage between Virginia and New England. It was worth the few thousand feet of rough water to get to the relative safety of Long Island Sound, safety also being money. The Narrows had its own perils: shoals, shifting sand bars, Atlantic storms, and no harbors to retreat to other than the bays behind the barrier islands, too shallow and uncertain. At Hell Gate, an unfavorable tide meant you had to wait. The choice came down to time and distance, which was money. A favorable tide was a good sign. So were favorable winds.

Piloting services provided expert advice and assistance: men with long experience escorting your ship to guide you through the rocks and tables.

Piloting services have a long history at Hell Gate, maybe the encounter between Dermer and the Lenape (who drew Dermer a map) being the first episode. In her book, *The Perils of the Port of New York*, Jeanette Rattray devotes a chapter to the Hell Gate pilots whose route ran "from Execution Rocks . . . ten miles to Hell Gate, and nineteen miles more to the Battery." The pilots were the true experts at reading water, the ones called on to assist even the most desperate: in the words of one pilot, the few "fly-by-night, underpowered, underequipped" operators too careless or ignorant of the dangers.

The most widely told story of ship against rock is that of the British twenty-eight-gun frigate, *HMS Hussar*, known within the context of Hell Gate, and melodramatically, as the "treasure ship." In November, 1780, the *Hussar* arrived in New York to load provisions before sailing on to Newport, Rhode Island. What the Hussar took on is not entirely clear. Certainly some dispatches intended for British Admiral Mariot Arbuthnot, stationed at Gardiner's Bay on Long Island to monitor French fleets—tensions were high in the city despite its being under British control. Such tensions might have impelled the British to relocate a rather sizable payroll in the form of gold bullion and coins to be distributed to its soldiers. The *Hussar*, commanded by Captain Charles Maurice Pole, was to leave New York by continuing north on the East River and out through Long Island Sound, a route that would take it through Hell Gate.

Pole, aware of the Gate's reputation, decided to call for a pilot who could handle what would be a difficult passage. The pilot sent to him was a slave named Swan, who belonged to the Hunt family, who had large holdings in Morrisania (in what is now the South Bronx). Swan, who had experience in negotiating vessels through the Gate, examined the *Hussar*, estimated its weight, and advised that the ship not sail. Being a slave, he had little say in the matter. Pole ordered the ship to shove off, and soon it was making its way upriver, Swan impressed into duty as the pilot. Sailing was uneventful until of course they reached Hell Gate. One particular rock—Pot Rock, off Hallett's Point—was especially dangerous because it was barely submerged, even at low water. To its side was a whirlpool called the Pot. Losing control as it tried to negotiate the Pot, the *Hussar* slammed Pot Rock with enough force to breach its hull.

Taking on water, the ship became captive to the flood tide and drifted farther to the north through the Hell Gate channel. Legend has it that the pilot, Swan, sensing a lost cause, dove off and swam ashore. A certain Captain Randall, witnessing the goings-on from shore, sent a crew to the dying ship to help its men off. The *Hussar* continued to drift helplessly, its profile steadily diminishing. Somewhere off the Brothers Islands, north of the channel, to this day no one knows exactly where, the *Hussar* sank.

Its treasure, if it existed, has never been found. Pole himself claimed that none existed. With its sinking, the Hussar entered history and legend, a cautionary tale to those unready for Hell Gate. It is remembered chiefly for its putative treasure—to this day, dreamers plan expeditions to find it—but the true nature of its mission and events surrounding the case remain murky, the facts apparently having gone down with the ship.

The *Hussar* is merely the most famous of wrecks, and that for its unfound treasure more than its sinking. But there were many others, ordinary working ships not so famous, caught in the same predicament of tide and boil. In the clipped language of a harbormaster's blotter, Jeanette Rattray lists a parade of calamity:

December, 1833. The sloop *Irene* struck the rocks at "Hurl Gate." Went to pieces.

November, 1849. The sloop *Dispatch* of Cold Spring Harbor, L.I., struck Pot Rock going through Hell Gate; Capt. John Mahan killed by blow from tiller.

September 19, 1860. The schooner *Margaret Dill*; Capt. Dill, from Windsor, N.S., with a load of plaster for New York, went ashore at Mill Rock, Hell Gate, yesterday. She will have to discharge her cargo before getting off.

December 8, 1864. The schooner *William Penn*, bound from New Haven to New York capsized, Hell Gate; Captain Stevens drowned.

August 13, 1865. Sloop *Planter* of Sag Harbor, Capt. Williams, cargo bone dust; total loss at Hallett's Point at Hell Gate; crew escaped.

November 3, 1865. Schooner *Chief* . . . run into at Hell Gate; sunk.

July 3, 1866. Schooner *Exchange* . . . wrecked at Hell Gate.

July 23, 1867. Sloop *Vienna* . . . sunk at Hell Gate.

July 28, 1867. Schooner *L. B. Ogden* . . . sunk at Hell Gate.

May 15, 1868. Schooner *E. C. Knight* . . . sunk at Hell Gate.

September 5, 1868. Schooner *Washington* . . . sunk at Hell Gate.

September 20, 1868. Sloop *Ethan Allen* . . . sunk off Blackwell's Island.

1871. Fall River liner *Providence*; Capt. Brayton, aground. August 3, 1871, collided in Long Island Sound with schooner *McComb* and unknown schooner. . . . October 15, 1872, collided with drilling machine at Hell Gate.

July 18, 1871. Schooner *Oscar E. Acken* . . . run into at Hell Gate by steamer Elm City; *Acken* sunk.

August 21, 1871. Schooner *Juno* ran on Gridiron, Hell Gate; took fire, total loss.

September 28, 1871. Steam tug *Delaware* struck by Astoria ferry *Williamsburg*; sunk in Pot Cove; port side stove in; pilot house carried away.

May 2, 1872. Schooner *William R. Knapp* run into by steamer *City of Hartford* between Hell Gate and Astoria, L.I., sank; cook drowned.

May 6, 1872. Schooner *Trimmer*, cargo lumber, struck Hell Gate, filled; beached by steam tug *Joe*, Astoria.

May 10, 1872. Schooner *William Butman* . . . struck reef at Hell Gate; sunk.

July 20, 1872. Schooner *Diadem* run into at Hell Gate by the steamer *Galatea*. The *Diadem* sank in minutes in the middle of the ship channel.

August 2, 1872. *George B. Bloomer*; filled and rolled over.

September 20, 1872: The *Diadem* wreck struck by the schooner *Flagg*; capsized.

May 13, 1873. Steamer *Hope* run into by steamer *Americus* at Hell Gate; *Hope* cut in two; 4 drowned.

September 7, 1873. Steam tug *Vixen* run into by *SS Granite State*; cut in two; sunk; Capt. Perkins drowned, engineer badly hurt.

February 18, 1874. Barge *Joseph E. Dow*; cargo ice for Brooklyn; ashore on Gridiron, Hell Gate.

March 20, 1874. Schooner *Elizabeth B.*, cargo coal, went ashore at Hallett's Point, Hell Gate; filled.

August 22, 1874. Schooner *Martha Jane* struck a rock in Hell Gate; filled.

November 17, 1874. Steam tug *Lilly* blew up at Hell Gate; sank.

December, 1874. Schooner *Fanny Fern* sunk at Hell Gate. She was raised and taken to Hallett's Cove. Later she was being towed through Hell Gate alongside the tug *D.S. Stetson* when she slewed onto Middle Ground, knocking a hole in her bottom. The tug cast off its towlines and refused to render assistance. The *Fanny Fern* sank in twenty minutes.

November, 1910. A four-masted freighting schooner, *Emily Baxter*, foundered and turned onto its keel. The captain and a mate managed to hang on and climb the keel. The captain was also a minister who had long intended to convert the mate, who made a habit of drinking as soon as he was ashore. Sitting on the keel, waiting for help, the captain saw his chance: "Now is the time to pray." The mate: "Hell, Captain, now is the time to swim."

One of the perils of Hell Gate, as this list shows, was the traffic. Not only did you have to watch for rocks and eddies and steer yourself clear, you had to watch for other ships who were also watching for rocks and eddies, and to get out of their way, you had to watch that they didn't steer themselves into you. In the aggregate, these calamities sound like a comedy of errors, and one wreck like any other. Not quite. For the individuals who went through a wreck, a run-in, a capsizing, or a rollover, each was its own catastrophe.

Unbarring

In mythology, rocks were mutable, thwarting, alive. At Hell Gate, they wouldn't get out of the way. Ships of larger berth and draught could not

make it through the narrow passage. Long experience with rocks and current begat a shared learning among mariners, but systematic knowledge was
lacking. No one knew exactly how to solve the problem because the problem
was not completely known: no one had ever done a survey of Hell Gate.
That changed in 1847 when a Coast Survey was organized under Alexander
Bache. Lieutenant Charles H. Davis conducted the survey and reported a
description of the rocks and currents. He also suggested a plan for blasting,
but the glacial pace of politics and Congress's inability to decide anything
led to another survey, this one done under the direction of Lieutenant David
Porter.

Porter's survey had one immediate benefit: a lovely and meticulous map,
the Coast Survey of 1851, showing the outlines of Hell Gate, the rocks within,
their location, the river's depth soundings, three shipping lanes (which made
the chart of Hell Gate look something like that of a railroad yard with lines
diverging at one end and converging at the other), and a number of shore-
side landmarks. In the middle of Hell Gate Basin, the cluster of rocks were
collectively called the Middle Reef, and within this cluster were a number of
smaller clusters and individual rocks: Flood Rock and the Gridiron among
them; also, Hen and Chickens, Negro Head, and Little Negro Head.

To the northeast, nearer to Ward's Island, were Frying Pan, Holmes Rock,
and the Hog Back. In Pot Cove between Hallett's Point and Ward's Island
were Ways Reef, the Shelldrake, and sitting right in the midst of the channel, Pot Rock, which doomed the *Hussar*. At low water, Pot Rock came to
within eight feet of the surface, but it acted like a dam, about 130 feet long,
and broadside to the current. Frying Pan was a narrow ledge, about nine feet
from the surface, and part of a chain running north-south from Hog Back
to Hallett's Point. Porter considered this rock among the most difficult to
remove. Way's Reef comprised two rocks, one conical and the other about
twenty yards to the north, a flatbed about ten feet square—particularly dangerous with a strong current running over it.

Fanning around Hallett's Point was the table Hallett's Reef. Below the
Point was a little rock known as Baldheaded Billy, a rounded top and exposed
at highwater. To the northwest of Middle Reef were Great and Little Mill
Rock, Heeltap Rock, and off the edge of 90th Street, another table called
Rhinelander Reef.

How the rocks were given their names and who named them is a matter of speculation: mariner talk and shipboard slang reflecting various adventures, apprehensions, sea life, jokes, localisms, barbarisms—names given and the best of them entering legend. Let's call these reasonable guesses:

- Pot Rock and Cove for the surrounding whirlpool
- Heeltap Rock after the kind of ship or the shoe
- Hog Back for its shape reminiscent of a hog, or a reference to the islands where hogs were kept, the surrounding waters being a fence
- Shell Drake for the thousands of ducks that took up residence there
- Holmes Rock perhaps for a captain named Holmes who accidentally smashed into it and whose name was thereafter attached by his associates who would never let him live it down
- Gridiron and Frying Pan, major chunks of unforbearance, for hell fire, for hellishness and churlishness, meant to mock or appease. Perhaps one suggested the other; and throw in Pot Rock, we have a set of three. Or perhaps the name Frying Pan followed that of the shoals of the same name in North Carolina.
- Baldheaded Billy, for the sleekness of its wet, rounded crown, "bald" being a common name for islands or rocks without vegetation. From a distance it appeared as a submerged albeit gigantic head.
- And, of course, a number of smaller rocks littering the Gate were judged unworthy of naming and on the map were labeled accordingly:

> . . . rock . . .   . . . rock . . .
>   . . . rock . . .
> . . . rock . . .   . . . rock . . .   . . . rock . . .
>   . . . rock . . .
> . . . rock . . .   . . . rock . . .
>   . . . rock . . .

One other set of rocks is worth noting: the Bread and Cheese, a small outcropping off the northern tip of Blackwell's (now Roosevelt) Island, and the site of another Hell Gate legend: a small fort, this one belonging not to the military but to the fort's builder and henceforth caretaker, one Thomas

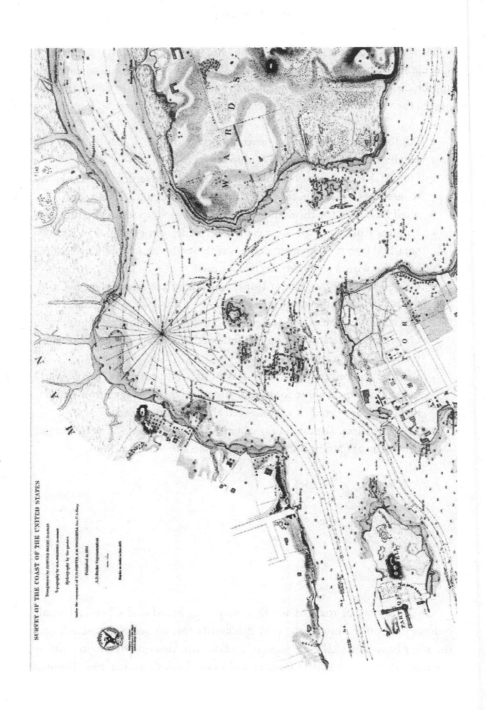

SURVEY OF THE COAST OF THE UNITED STATES

Maxey. The fort was his idea to defend the island against a possible British invasion. This was about 1865, but Maxey was presumably Irish, and fighting the long war. To build the fort, Maxey used materials found nearby: clay, rock, dirt, and tall grasses. To get the materials to the construction site, he faced an engineering challenge: the watery gap between island and outcropping. He solved his problem by creating a landfill using the clay, till, and rock. Power was supplied by his own brute strength and intelligence, working alone and by his own hand. It took determination, imagination, and time. But time was something Tom Maxey had in spades, as he was an inmate at the Lunatic Asylum, located just down the road from the fort. His fort became his home, at least part time, and one can imagine him alone inside or out in his garden, also part of his fort, enjoying his measure of peace.

The solitary engineering activities of Tom Maxey aside, nothing could defeat the rocks save obliteration. In 1851, a French engineer named Benjamin Maillefert, who specialized in underwater demolition, stepped forward and offered to unbar the Gate by means of placing explosives underwater against the rock, which would then be shattered by the concussion. In August 1851, he knocked off about four feet of Pot Rock, results encouraging enough to warrant additional expense. But work proceeded piecemeal. In March of 1852, an accident resulted in the maiming of Maillefert and the deaths of three of his assistants. Maillefert was undeterred. In August 1852, he succeeded in knocking more off Pot Rock and some of Shell Drake. "Hell Gate has lost its terrors!" he exclaimed. Not quite. Maillefert continued, but funding was drying up.

The political turmoil of the 1850s and then the Civil War brought a temporary halt to work at Hell Gate.

Meanwhile, Lieutenant General John Newton had been charged to deal with the problem of the rocks. He hired Sidney F. Shelbourne, whose idea was to float a rig above the rock from which demolition could proceed. He had minor success, until his rig was hit, in succession, by a tug, then a brig, then a canal boat. His contract, which had already been extended, had only three days to go. Maillefert returned, rehired by Newton. But his methods of blowing the tops off the rock proved costly and inefficient. Maillefert's career at Hell Gate came to an end. The *New York Times* wrote in his obituary: "Prof. Maillefert since then led a quiet life, not engaging in any business."

Newton lamented the waste of time.

Newton was methodical, a systems man. Demolition work, he realized, would require stability, which water could not provide, especially at Hell Gate. Studying the problem, he realized that if real progress was to be made, he would have to go into the bedrock, obdurate but stable, and blast it away to create "subaqueous tunnels." These would be elaborate works of construction, hollowed earthen corridors, the rock walls to be drilled with holes enough to accommodate miles of charge wire and tons of explosives. It would take years, but it would be thorough. Not all explosives would require a charge. Several could be wired, and the rest would react "sympathetically."

Hallett's Point had a particularly obstreperous block. A long spur jutted against Hallett's Point projected out far enough into the river to throw the ebb tide onto the nearby Gridiron, where it broke violently. This spur would be the first to go. The plan was to erect a coffer dam outside the shipping lanes, dig a pit, and then drill tunnels—"headings"—fanning out from the pit, which would be connected by other transverse tunnels—"galleries." Ultimately, these tunnels would be blown up, the debris settling into the underground chambers and either carted away or left to fill the hollow.

From time to time visitors were allowed to tour the work site and the tunnels below, public relations being important, and among one group was journalist James Richardson, who later published an account of the tour in Scribner's Magazine, "The Unbarring of Hell Gate." Host and guide of the tour was the superintendent of the operation, G.C. Reitheimer, a German engineer, experienced and long renowned. To get to his office, visitors traversed a causeway built from a pile of boulders from Fort Stevens, at Hallett's Point, which by this time is a ruin. Superintendent Reitheimer maintained a collection of curios and souvenirs from past projects, his desk a reliquary of natural objects, including many rocks: quartz, gneiss, mica schist, "rusty and rotten . . . you can crumble it in your hand. A month hence it will be hard as granite." Also examples of *teredo navalis*, the shipworm whose physiognomy suggested the means to bore tunnels through rock.

The visitors watched as ships passed by: tugs, coasters, passenger vessels. One of the latter got caught in a whirlpool in Pot Cove and was swung around—only by means of a sudden and fortuitous breeze could the helmsman regain control. Here was evidence of the benefit of the blasting work done over the previous years: had Professor Maillefert not blasted away the top of Pot Rock, the vessel might have gone the way of the *Hussar*. Other ships were not as lucky: one had gone aground at the Gridiron the night before, its cargo of lime catching fire and leaving the ship a charred crisp.

Visitors climbed into a car for the descent into the headings and galleries. At bottom was a gaggle of miners waiting to return to the surface—Cornish miners, the only ones willing to put up with the wet and sloppy conditions of the rock tunnels: wet always, and in winter thin sheets of ice would form on their jackets. Much of the rock was a dark hornblendic gneiss. Dripping water produced striped stains of slime and vegetation, rusted yellow oxide. In the galleries, named for American luminaries—Jefferson, Madison, Franklin, Jackson, Grant—work proceeded slowly and cautiously. Each heading might reveal different strata of rock, and the composition and lay of each had to be understood before drilling. Soundings were taken to distinguish bedrock from mere boulders, not to mention organic matter and the odious outflow of sewer pipes. Work proceeded nonstop in three shifts of eight hours, tripling what could be accomplished in a typical work day. When the project started, drilling had been done by hand, but later, drills powered by compressed air and fitted with diamond heads were used. Holes were drilled and set with small charges of nitroglycerin. Water was a constant problem. More than once, seams opened and allowed a seepage (sometimes a rush) of river water, to be caulked with dry wood, or in the case of bigger seams, bags of clay. At times, the direction of headings would have to be altered because the rock was too seamy, too susceptible to total and premature collapse.

One of the party, a brewer, had a special appreciation of these chambers, seeing other possibilities. "What a splendid place for storing lager bier!" he exclaimed. The chambers, artificial caverns that did indeed resemble wine or beer cellars, were as high as fifty feet in some places, an impressive sight: commodious, dark, and wet. Darkness was alleviated in the galleries and headings by bands of bright light, flecks of mica in the walls that reflected sunlight. Where strata were vertical, the walls were smooth, and succumbed easily to the miners' work.

Preparing for a new blast in the walls, workers removed the staging material and put tools out of the way of exploding rock; except for a small detonat-
ing crew, all miners exited the shaft.

It took seven years of preparation to ready Hallett's Reef for its ultimate
demolition, in 1876. Ten headings were dug. The final blast required seven
thousand holes in the tunnels packed with thirty thousand pounds of explosives. It took another six years to clear away the ninety thousand tons of
debris, deepening the channel by twenty-six feet.

The other reefs and rock clusters were done the same way: years of digging labyrinthine tunnels. The coup de grace was Flood Rock, the largest of
the Hell Gate tables, 1,200 by 650 feet, but which showed only 230 square
feet of itself above water. Demolition took nine years of preparation. Fifty-five
thousand explosives were used, only three thousand of which would be set to
explode, the remainder to be tripped by "sympathy." Finally, on October 10,
1885, with over fifty thousand spectators present to witness the event—it had
been well publicized—the now General Newton signaled his eleven-year-old
daughter to push the plunger that would set off the detonation. First came a
low, jarring rumble, and then nine acres of the river's surface lifted. Geysers
of rock and water erupted skyward 150 feet, an explosion that registered on
seismographs as far south as Princeton, New Jersey.

The rocks in fact are not all gone. Mill Rock remains the most visible vestige. At the start of the War of 1812, the army built a blockhouse on Great
Mill Rock, near the west shipping lane. In 1821, it burned, and over the next
several decades became a pirates' haunt and squatters den. In 1850, an enter-
prising fellow named John Clark declared squatters' rights and took the island
as his own. On his island he built a tavern, which became a regular stop for
sailors. Reputedly, Clark served a mean clam chowder.

Detritus from Flood Rock was used to connect Great Mill Rock with Little
Mill Rock, thereafter known simply as Mill Rock. Hog Back is still where it
always was, just off the shore of Ward's Island. A couple of pinnacles jut above
surface just off Astoria. Other rocks still exist at the edges, as do the hidden
reefs, safely submerged. Their names still appear on nautical charts, partly in
homage and partly because some are still a force to reckon with. Other rocks
linger where they always were, ghostly presences. The most wicked currents
still appear above where Flood Rock once was.

Excursion

A rowing mate tells me of a ship that burned.

"The *Slocum*," I tell her.

"Are you going to put it in the book?"

Many ships caught fire and burned; boilers exploded. This of course happened everywhere, not just at Hell Gate. The cause? Nascent technology, few precautions, lax standards, and safety an afterthought, if a thought at all. In December, 1880, the steam tug *L. Markle* blew up and sank off Randall's Island. In June of that year, the *Seawanakha* and the *Sylvan Dell* were racing up the East River when the *Seawanakha* caught fire and was grounded off Ward's Island. Doctors and staff of the Metropolitan Hospital rushed to aid the victims. While the *Seawanakha* was passing through the channel, witnesses watched as passengers jumped overboard to escape the fire, only to be sucked into the rotating paddle wheels, which clubbed them to death. In 1932, the *Observation* exploded, killing dozens of iron and construction workers. It could have been any of these or others that my rowing mate was referring to when she mentioned a ship that had burned, but I knew she meant the *Slocum*.

"The *Slocum*. Yes, the women and children. It happened here, so it has to go into the book."

For once, Hell Gate was blameless—not the cause of death, but a presence over it nonetheless, a geographical specter.

On June 15, 1904, a thousand women and children from St. Mark's German Lutheran Church in the Kleindeutschland ("Little Germany") section of the lower East Side boarded the paddle-wheel steamer *General Slocum* for a day's outing at Locust Grove on the shores of Long Island Sound. For many, especially the children, it was a new experience, a passage to a bright country, which was to them a new land, and not just a day in the country, but a trip on a paddle-wheel steamer—and what a steamer! The *Slocum* was grand and colorful, 235 feet long, with huge paddle-wheels on either side. The captain, William van Schaick, was a veteran of steamship service: responsible and serious. Despite some scrapes over his career, he had never lost a boat or passenger.

At 9:30 in the morning, the *Slocum* pulled away from the East Third Street pier and began its sail upriver. It was a glorious morning, warm and clear ("severe clear"), salty breezes blowing back mothers' bonnets, river spray sparkling in the sun, and the great paddlewheels churning water into foam.

While the steamer was churning toward Hell Gate, a boy noticed a small fire in a lower hold and reported it to a ship's mate. The mate dismissed him. Other passengers also thought they detected fire; they saw smoke coming from the lower deck, but this was attributed to chowder being cooked in the galley.

At first, the fire was confined to the forward of the ship. Here was a storeroom for rope, canvas, rags—flammables.

Then came a muffled explosion, and a sheet of flame engulfed the forward. The flame spread quickly, and passengers were forced to the stern.

People on shore could not believe what they were seeing—passengers at the stern enjoying themselves, oblivious to the panic at the prow. The people on shore waved frantically, hopelessly. They shouted to the passengers to get off, their voices drowned out by the currents.

And once passengers realized the danger they were in, where could they go? Into the river.

Within minutes the entire ship was ablaze. The *Slocum* was equipped with life-preservers, but they were made of cork. Years old and untested, the cork preservers were now dried and rotted: useless. Those who strapped them on and jumped hit the water and sank almost immediately. In the words of *Slocum* historian Edward O'Donnell: "splash . . . splash . . . nothing."

Women grabbed their children and leapt into the water. Others were trapped inside. A boy climbed a pole. When the pole broke, he fell into the fire.

People were confused, running, panicked, not knowing which way to die. Children were sought, names shouted and re-shouted, but shouts went unanswered or unheard amid the screams and the sound of fire.

Rescuers rowed out to save everyone they could. It was said that some men in boats rowed toward women flailing in the water, reached for their hands, then stripped their wrists of their jewelry and rowed back to shore.

Others claimed to have seen a yachtsman who happened to be in the channel and witnessed the scene. Once he'd had enough entertainment, he sailed away, leaving the chaos in his wake.

Captain Van Schaick hesitated to turn the ship toward shore, fearing the fire might spread to nearby oil tanks. Instead he allowed the boat to drift upstream, its plumes of smoke ascending at a constant rate from its inexhaustible source below. The *Slocum* drifted until it finally ran aground in the flats off North Brother Island.

At North Brother Island, hospital patients in the confines of their beds could tell something was happening and shrieked when they looked out their windows to see what it was. Their shrieks confused their attendants until they too went to the windows and looked.

The beach became an impromptu morgue, bodies being taken from the river and draped with sheets, and then neatly lined up on the beach. Family members, fathers mostly, were allowed to walk up and down the line to find their loved ones, and if they wanted to look, it was up to them to lift the sheet, take a quick look, and then let the sheet drop. The line was long, but it moved. *No, she's not the one. Next. No, she's not the one. Next.*

Some survivors returned that night on the el train, a night like any other, and walked home.

Children who did not die were put on the el and left to find their own way home.

Where was everyone else?

The *Slocum* has been remembered intermittently, most often after various disasters propel it into newspaper sidebars, and most recently after September 11, 2001. In our fetish to list and liken, we insert the *Slocum* near the World Trade Center and compare them: Before September 11, the *Slocum* was the worst single day of death in New York's history: 1,031 dead.

A psychic tie: leaflets displaying pictures and names of the missing from the World Trade Center, pasted to so many walls on New York, were not found on the *Slocum* memorial in Tompkins Square, in what was old Kleindeutschland. Newspapers in the days following the *Slocum* disaster included small photos: "Would you be so kind to let us know if you have seen this boy?"

Aftermath

At his trial, Captain Van Schaick was blamed because he was the convenient goat, and in being so convenient, he was sent to Sing Sing. He was later pardoned by President Taft and moved inland to Fulton County, New York, where he spent his remaining days in isolation on a farm.

The effect of the ship's sinking and the grief it caused in the living spread from Kleindeutschland to other parts of the city, including Yorkville, on the east side of Manhattan, just below Hell Gate, where the ship caught fire.

After the fire and its bestial half-sinking in the mud, the *Slocum* was rescued and refitted into a steamer barge. Rechristened the *Maryland*, it sailed for a few more years until it foundered and sank once again, this time in the Atlantic off the coast of New Jersey.

Met Him Pike Hoses

Catastrophes heard at a distance, a story at the margins: words intermingled among many others.

Dublin, June 16, 1904: Father John Conmee is walking along the North Strand Road, on his way to a hospital to see about a boy, recently orphaned, the son of Paddy Dignam, whose funeral is to take place today. He salutes a Mr. William Gallagher, who salutes back. From shops come the smell of "bacon and cools of butter." Father Conmee moves past Grogan's, whose tobacco shop displays signboards of today's news, yesterday's events, including an announcement of a "dreadful catastrophe in New York."

Years after the *Slocum* came to rest in the mudflats off North Brother Island, it came to rest in the pages of James Joyce's Odyssean novel, *Ulysses*. Joyce included *Slocum* references because he had to: the fictive day of *Ulysses*, the day of Paddy Dignam's funeral, is the day after the *Slocum* burned. In the novel's real-time world, it is not unusual that the citizens of Dublin on their rounds about the city are passing and noting the previous day's events written on signboards placed outside of newsstands, messages beamed across the North Atlantic of a city in its agitation. Joyce mentions the incident numerous times in the book, often casually, as news of the day: Father Conmee reading the signboard, and another that mentions a "New York disaster. One thousand dead." A typist in a newspaper office types: June 16, 1904. Joyce uses the *Slocum* story in part to set his fictive day, making scattered references to the month, day, and year for readers to put together like a puzzle. The *Slocum* is one more piece of dating.

But not only that: the *Slocum* is also a source of casual barroom conversation in the novel. In the Wandering Rocks episode, at Mr. Crimmins's pub,

Mr. Kernan, ordering a gin, breaks into casual mention of the lovely weather, how good it is for the country, and maybe it will help stave off the complaints of the farmers, who are always complaining. He goes on, making conversation of the news of the day, anything to fill the air: "Terrible affair, that General *Slocum* explosion. Terrible, terrible! A thousand casualties. And heartrending scenes." A comment on America: "Things like this are always happening in America . . . sweepings of every country including our own." (Wonder if the *New York Times* was a source for Joyce: "Scenes terrible . . . heartbreak," the *Times'* account read. Meanwhile, the Irish *Freeman's Journal*, which Joyce almost certainly used as a source, attributed the *Slocum's* sinking to being hemmed in by the rocks at Hell Gate—and it used Hell Gate by name, which Joyce did not.)

The *Slocum* tragedy also fit into Joyce's symbolic scheme that pervades the thinking of its protagonist, Leopold Bloom, as he moves through his day. "Met him pike hoses" is a reference to an earlier episode in the book, in which Bloom's wife Molly is reading a book, *Ruby: the Pride of the Ring*, a book about a circus. Bloom's thoughts are on the action within the ring, something of a horror show in itself, and also on the crowd witnessing the goings-on: "Cruelty behind it all. Doped animals . . . had to look the other way. Mob gaping. Break your neck and we'll break our sides. Families of them." (Cruelty . . . had to look the other way . . . mob gaping—equally a description of those lined along a shore watching a drifting burning ship.)

Molly asks her husband about a word she doesn't understand: "Met him pike hoses," she pronounces it.

"Met him what?"

This time she points to the word, her lacquered nail isolating it within the text. He looks: "Metempsychosis . . . that means the transmigration of souls."

Her impatience is evident: "O, rocks! Tell us in plain words."

Later, Bloom is walking past Doran's pub. He helps a young blind man cross a street, brooding on the man's affliction and the afflictions of others, and the victims of the *Slocum* come to mind: "All those women and children excursion beanfest burned and drowned in New York. Holocaust."

The *Slocum* incident is a nautical reference, a shipwreck. *Ulysses*, like its source, the *Odyssey*, abounds in nautical references—its very thread is a navigation. As Robert Tracy points out in "All Them Rocks in the Sea," his study of Irish sea tales ("immrama") and *Ulysses*, "Frequent reminders of the sea emphasize the voyage theme of *Ulysses*," from the book's opening at the Martello Tower on the Irish Sea; to the return of the sailor D.B. Murphy, "tired of all them rocks"; to the *Slocum*. The references to Bloom and Murphy (and Odysseus) are to those who eventually return home; the reference to the *Slocum* is to the thousand who do not. Bloom's speculations and musings about transmigration and souls carry deeper into Karma, the visitation of sins of the past into the lives of the present, and to the Greeks, for whom souls become trees, natural objects. The *Slocum* is an instance of wandering in a book of wanderings, of transit. And could it be that these innocents were the ones chosen for earlier transgressions? Perhaps, if you believe in Karma. Bloom muses, thinking of the blind man: "Where is the justice being born that way?"

Catastrophes have a long arc: the suddenness of the event, the innocence of the victims, the scale of loss, the impress of a single day on the remainder of everyone's days, the emotional upheaval in those left behind, the injunction to never forget, the widening gap between then and now, the forgetting.

CHAPTER 6

Riverrun

Down by the Old Hell Hole

For reasons I have never understood, portals are not only places of transit but also places of momentary congregation, stoppage. How many times have I come to a doorway only to have to wend my way around a group of people who have chosen that spot to stop and chat? Such walkarounds are easy enough, but also pointless: I find myself mouthing the usual barbarities: "Why here? Get out of the way!" When space outside can be used as a waystation, why choose the narrows as the place to halt? Perhaps it is coincidence that two parties simultaneously flow from opposite ends only to meet at a portal. Or are portals of symbolic importance, becoming chance meeting grounds, places of decision: to go this way or that, or to go or not to go at all?

From across the whitecaps comes a squadron of kayaks, beating across the ship channel toward Ward's Island, and with some purpose: to get away from the sludge vessel coming from behind them. The flood current is manageable, and the kayakers haven't worked up much of a sweat. They pull up to shore, and their leader unfolds a laminated navigational chart to see where they are. "Ahoy," I say. He looks up at me as though I've lost my marbles. "Where you headed?" I ask. "Around Manhattan, to the Hudson River," he says. "To your left," I tell him, as though he has asked for directions. They head out again, just as the wake of the sludge vessel passes under them. They roll with it, use it to propel themselves; "surfing a wake," it is called, and it means what you would think.

No one comes to stay at Hell Gate; no one docks for good. It is a gate, to be passed through: "transited." There are few landings to speak of along the shore, and what piers are left are taken over immediately by fishermen.

Stories of Hell Gate are centered not on voyages but on transits: everyone is bound elsewhere, movement through portals, from city to sea, from sea back to safe harbor. Sometimes these ships in transit look positively lost, like the giant Japanese container ship—the Kiso Maru, I think it was—which one evening came through the Gate from the Sound instead of going the long way around Montauk and through the Narrows. It was a tight fit. Everyone onshore stopped and looked. Godzilla herself wouldn't have been more improbable.

For a few evenings running, I got serious about the water, going down to the river to watch the currents, this time to make measurements, estimate current velocity, marking time and place. I intended to compare my observations to the nautical charts, to determine if what I saw with my own eyes correlated to the charts—not to prove the charts correct but to test my own powers of observation against hidden realities. The tide was ebbing on these succeeding evenings, flowing at a good clip, the streams of currents flowing through stilled water. Winds produced whitecaps, and on the whole, the vista and smells before me were of the sea. Images piled: in the distance, the sun's reflection off the anchorage of the Hell Gate Bridge cast a likeness of a Viking ship in the water. The sun reflected very white. These sorts of distractions interfered with my science. Small, undulating whirlpools, hundreds of them, formed and vanished near the shore walls. I theorized that the rough patch of water just off Horns Hook during an ebb current was the epicenter of a disruption deep below, the remains of Middle Reef.

The charts and tables I use are from a variety of sources: newspapers, NOAA tide tables, a manual called *Eldridge Tide and Pilot*, with its distinctive yellow cover. *Eldridge* contains a series of charts for New York harbor showing current direction and speed at one-hour intervals following high water and low water at the Battery. Mariners use these charts to predict the best time to sail in New York harbor. An inset in each chart magnifies Hell Gate so that the complex currents in and out of its arms and through its basin can be shown clearly. Action here is complex. The rising tide on the Eastern seaboard enters New York harbor and splits at the lower tip of Manhattan: one current up the Hudson and the other up the East River. The Hudson current also wraps around the top of Manhattan at Spuyten Duyvel and descends through the Harlem River to the Hell Gate Basin. When water is high at the Battery, and

for an hour or so later, the flow is still in flood stage. This direction changes in less than two hours: the flow is now an ebb into Hell Gate, not yet strong, but gaining all the while. For the next three hours or so, the ebb begins to assert itself: this is the start of the current that entered the harbor hours ago and has now traveled around Long Island and is returning via the Sound. At different points during this cycle, currents have advanced in and out of the Harlem River, have twisted through the basin and around Mill Rock. Six hours and minutes after the start of one cycle, the currents slacken and then reverse themselves. Depending on the prevailing winds and the weather and the phase of the moon, the currents can be less vicious or more. The worst usually comes toward the end of the cycle; especially at the end of the ebb, the current can achieve five or more knots. But this is only the general tendency; particulars depend on those exact winds and weather, the exact phase of the moon, the exact location of your vessel.

The best demonstration I saw of the currents came early one winter morning at Horns Hook, and came with the visible help of huge ice chunks and plates floating upriver in a flood of about four knots or so. The major part of this floe headed out through the basin and east toward the Gate, but another floe had broken away and pushed itself into Hell Gate Bay. Further up, past Mill Rock, still another flow had broken away and headed landward toward Manhattan. Since it had nowhere to go, it circled south and then met up with the floe heading north. Both were equally strong, and began to jostle each other like crowds transiting through turnstiles, each moving toward its own return in a slow circuit of Hell Gate Bay.

During these outings on the water, I watched ships as well, and pleasure craft, which transit mostly in summer. Small motorized craft have it easy; they are nimble, quick, and can turn on a dime. But in the East River they mix with all manner of working and official vessels: oilers, tugs pushing or pulling barges, Coast Guard boats, NYPD, FDNY, sludge vessels from the Department of Environmental Protection. Working craft know no season. Three DEPs in particular make regular transits through the Gate: the North River, the Newtown Creek, and the Red Hook. Their job is to transport liquid waste to the wastewater treatment plant on Randall's Island, another found use for that multifaceted island. Their hulls are a light gray, their logo DEP in red and blue, and rust spots indicate long hours spent in the water with whatever maintenance is required to keep them in working order. Transits through the Gate look simple. Ships come in, and ships go out. None seems to have trouble; all motor through gracefully—as simple as passing through an open door. Or so it appears from shore. Ships no longer need to swing wide to the west, and given their size and velocity, they cannot; nor do they need to hug the Astoria shore on the eastern side.

A black and white and gray day, the river in flood cycle, heading uptown. A tow and barge push upriver, the correct terminology: eastbound for the Gate. I catch sight of them while they are still just this side of the Queensborough Bridge. They are by now "committed to the transit," a phrase that implies a brink past which there is no return and no stopping. Though the nautical hazards of the rocks are gone, modern shipmasters know that Hell Gate still has hidden dangers, its transit requiring precaution and intelligence. Daniel Denton spoke of Hell Gate as presenting little difficulty to those mariners "well acquainted," but he did not mention the experience needed to gain that acquaintance.

These terms and phrases I use when speaking of ship movements—"transit," "eastbound for the Gate," "committed"—I get from Captain Bill Brucato. In the

Hell Gate pages of his *New York Tugmasters Weblog,* Captain Brucato describes what it takes to become acquainted, what to watch for, what to know. He admonishes to think before doing, and how to think before doing becomes an undoing. His blog falls into a tradition of navigational manuals called *peripli*— Latinized from a Greek word meaning "sailing around"—practical manuals to guide mariners as they sail along coastlines from port to port. He writes for professionals, but even we amateur water-watchers might learn something. I found his blog because I was looking for something of the contemporary.

The tug with barge is now creeping past Roosevelt Island, steady and sure of itself, like a thousand other units I have seen come through here. I notice it is one of those notch configurations in which the tug's nose is in the butt of the barge it is pushing. I also notice behind it a second tug, without barge, which is following a couple of hundred feet or so behind in its wake. There is some turbulence, but nothing the units can't handle.

From *New York Tugmasters*:

> During a spring tide cycle the velocity for the ebb current can easily reach 5.0 knots or more depending on prevailing weather conditions. Wind from easterly weather will tend to increase tidal ranges and flow and cause tidal changes to occur later than expected, extended periods of west-north-westerly weather will hold levels below normal and cause tidal changes to occur earlier and with less velocity. It's just a function of geography and wind direction how the NY Upper Bay and Long Island Sound respond to the effects of wind.

Hell Gate has one more characteristic that adds to a shipmaster's difficulties: it turns not once but twice, eastbound, around Hallett's Point, and then northbound through the channel:

> The turn at Hallett's Point is the initial turn into Hell Gate proper and is usually "shaped up" by finding the center line of the Tri-Boro Bridge and sighting a safe distance off Negro Point and then splitting the difference for the left turn under the Tri-Boro and Hell's Gate Rail Bridges.

The key is balance:

If there is a significant amount of flood current left before slack, the eddies flowing from the Harlem River (from left to right approaching the point) will certainly slide the tow towards the Astoria side of the river once the left turn under the bridges is made. The port side is now broad to the current and its influence will require the helm to increase to a hard right rudder with a gentle increase of throttle until the tow has advanced past Negro Point and out of the cross-current. . . .

But screw it up:

. . . apply a hard right too quickly . . . or . . . if a throttle is slammed to the stops, the starboard push gear will be taking a huge load and it's possible that the gear could part and cease to be of use as the tow falls out of shape towards the rocky shoreline of the Astoria Wall.

And then . . . *bam.*

I have often seen ships appear to slide as they go into that turn and then disappear around Hallett's Point into Pot Cove—the infamous spot where the *Hussar* hit Pot Rock—but I have never seen a ship not reappear. I have also seen incoming ships appear to head for Mill Rock before turning south in what looks like a pivot, its stern sliding out farther than its prow. The tug and the lone tug that I've been following move into Pot Cove and disappear. Eventually, the tug and barge unit reappear to the north, but the lone tug does not. Not until the unit safely passes under the Triborough does the lone tug emerge from the cove behind the point, and then it makes an odd maneuver. It heads west toward Ward's Island, speeding close along its shoreline behind Mill Rock and then turns and heads back downriver in front of the rail from where I am watching. It's possible that the lone tug I was watching was acting as a pilot boat. Captain Brucato cites the navigational guide, *Coast Pilot,* which sizes up some of the general situation for Hell Gate, and then admonishes that for finer points one should consult local piloting services. In other words: we can take you only so far.

The Navy surveyors who produced the 1851 chart of Hell Gate included a legend at the bottom of the map, "Sailing Directions" (another periplus), which contains instructions for transiting the Gate from the east, from the west, in flood tide, in ebb tide. It speaks of hazards, and it too mentions land-marks to use in order to shape up the transit, landmarks that are long gone—a little white house at the edge of Ward's Island, the same house mentioned in the Rambler's story of potter's field. Between the 1851 "Sailing Directions" and Captain Brucato's blog all these years hence is a continuity of enter-at-your-own-risk at Hell Gate. Captain Brucato mentions a particularly large back eddy off the northern tip of Roosevelt Island that sets up at the ebb cycle, perhaps the same series of eddies depicted just off Hallett's Point on the 1851 map: a continuity of peril.

There are things the untrained eye misses, and even things the aware eye does not see but can only be felt by a body caught in the pull and drag of the water. I have never seen a ship founder, but despite the demolition of the rocks, they still do. Jeanette Rattray's stories of wreck and accident continued into the twentieth century:

> Summer of 1960: the tug *Devon* was carried by an ebb tide into the tanker Craig Reinauer, after its steering gear failed. The *Devon* sank off Hallett's Point but was later raised, refitted, and made operational.

> September 1963: the tugboat Flushing capsized and sank in 125 feet of water at Hell Gate. The captain, Charles L. Scouten, and three deckhands were lost. Six crew members were saved, including the cook, who could not swim but kept a life preserver handy at all times, picked up from the water by helicopter.

> Mar 12, 1969: the tug *Ocean Queen* was rammed by the *Four Lakes* just off East 90th Street. Captain Joseph Meier, 49, of the *Ocean Queen* was never seen again.

In 2011, a tug/barge unit ran aground on the Hog Back and had to be pushed off by other tugs working in tandem. Someone with a camera turned the mishap into entertainment (this is New York, after all) and put it out on YouTube. Someone added in the comments section: "50 yards from the end of a career." Captain Brucato tells of arriving at the Gate behind another unit and hearing over the radio of a barge that had come loose from its lines to the tug, drifted downstream banging off the sea walls, and came to rest only by crashing into another barge tied up somewhere in the East 60s. "Unforgiving": (another Brucato word): one mistake and there is no return. The truth about New York rivers is that they all can get ugly, not just Hell Gate, but Hell Gate resonates because Hell resonates. In fact, NOAA also publishes a chart of wrecks surveyed and marked on charts in New York harbor. It colors them blue. From a high enough perspective above the harbor, the water is all blue. These are not the historic wrecks of piratical and treasure-laden romance—most are the result of accidents, long forgotten.

I made something of an acquaintance of Captain Brucato through a brief correspondence. I had smaller matters in mind, phenomena I had observed from shore and could not explain: "What are those smooth undulating, almost glassy patches on the surface of the water?" I asked. "Generally round or oblong in shape . . . and though ripples form and break on the edges, they don't appear to be eddies." I hoped my lack of technical language in describing this phenomenon would not interfere with my meaning.

"The thing you are likely witnessing," Captain Brucato replied, "is an upwelling caused by inconsistencies in the river's bank or bottom. The deflection causes the current to flow up toward the surface rather than along the bank. As we would call it, 'the tide is boiling.'" He went on: "For what it's worth, calling the current 'tide' is a misnomer, in the local vernacular which often calls it a fair tide (following), bucking tide (head current) or slack tide (no current)." (Vocabulary is the immediate pleasure of Captain Brucato's blog.) "Slack water can refer to the end of the rise and fall of the height of the tide, or the lack of velocity of the current while it changes direction. The duration of slack current in Hell Gate is measured in minutes as in five to ten minutes." The "Sailing Directions" of 1851 also noted the duration to be about six minutes. Continuity of peril: the basics of the system: the river goes in and then goes out, now as always, and for a brief interlude it is at peace.

Free Rowing, Tuesday Afternoons

The more I circled around Hell Gate, the more I knew I was creating a problem for myself. In thinking about my excursions I used a geometric image: walking the perimeter of a hole that exists in the midst of a city. It was a strategy that worked to a point. *Gat* is hole or mouth, a vortex, deep and dark, penetrable only at great risk. But, realistically, there was no reason why I couldn't traverse its mouth, something done every day by many, even if I kept to myself the idea that to traverse it is to tempt its guardians into swallowing me whole. There was nowhere left to go but to the water—a small boat would do.

To that end, I sought out boats or people with boats. I had kayaked before in the relative safety of Hallett's Cove, an easy introduction to the waters of the East River, but its smallness was constricting and—though I am hardly one to tempt fate—its mildness grew tiresome. At an art exhibit on Randall's Island, I found an artist, Marie Lorenz, who was offering free rides in small wooden boats of her own design and construction. "Part dory and part Whitehall gig," she said. I was among a small crew who navigated the west channel of the East River. We headed north toward the Bronx Kill, with the current, of course. On our way, near the section of the Triborough Bridge that joins Randall's Island to Manhattan, we passed through conflicting and swirling currents, one minute north, the next a crosscurrent west, the next against an eddy. Small and unthreatening, bare hints of the river's capriciousness. It was near high water. We hit a rock barely peeking above the surface of the river. There was no damage, but I thought us to have just symbolically associated ourselves with the mariners who sailed in the whistling straits that wrecked their boats and sent them to the bottom.

On the Bronx side of the Kill, we noticed the entrance to a narrow tunnel in the river bank, the mouth of some kind of discharge pipe. I expected a foul-smelling sewer; instead it was a pleasant and cool grotto, and judging by the brick tubular construction evidently quite old. It was a tight fit, but we were able to advance several feet. Absolute dark. Marie looked for eels. "A friend told me," she said, "that eels spawn at the same spot for hundreds of generations, so that if one spies an eel in one of these outflows, that is sufficient proof it was once a creek." We saw no eels, so there was no proof positive, but the absence of eels was neither proof negative. Later, I checked my 1909 map and saw a narrow blue rivulet marked at about this place on the Kill. Presumably, this is the very creek. No eels, but from the lack of sewage and strong odor it was clear that it was not a sewer. We had to back out by pushing against the brick walls.

But we never made it into the Gate, owing to lack of time and an opposing current.

I continued my search for boats. Various websites were of no value—dinner cruises or party boats, and all that they entail: the distractions of small talk and disco dancing in the moonlight, getting drunk in the sea breeze. I had read of a man who when the spirit moved him paddled his inflatable dinghy from City Island to Manhattan. That sounded more interesting, and I would gladly have made a small donation for a ride, but it was a story from years ago, and who knew if his dinghy was still seaworthy? It was then that I learned of a group who offered free rowing in the East River on Tuesday afternoons off 96th Street.

Free rowing! In a wooden boat, no less. And 96th Street was Hell Gate itself, or at least the bay leading to Hell Gate. I stopped by.

"Where do you go?" I asked a man who seemed to be in charge. "Around here," he said, waving his hand out toward the cove. "Do you ever go into Hell Gate?"

"Sure."

"When?"

"Depends."

"On what?"

"The tide."

Later, I found out his name was Phil Yee, and he was indeed in charge, along with his wife, Mary Nell Hawk. The group called themselves the East River Crew. They were of different backgrounds, trades, perspectives, interests, but all united in an appreciation of local waters and maritime activity. River sailors, I thought, and I thought with them I might achieve my ambitions. I signed on. I say "signed on" in that nautical sense of signing on with a ship, but really it was just a waiver that absolves the Crew from responsibility should your boat go down. I fitted myself with a life-jacket and was ready to go. It was later I found that their boats never go down.

Phil was a little testy that afternoon. A strong wind from the south was rippling through the cove, and most of his crew were inexperienced. Some were nervous; children clung to parents. My own fear was falling off the edge of the dock into the water, or worse, into the boat, several feet below topside. At least the water would provide a softer landing, and I can swim, but I imagined hitting the hard edge of wood would knock me silly. Phil shepherded us down the dock ladder and into the boat, which was rocking atop the rippling water. He cautioned us not to aggravate the rocking: "Be careful to step into the center of the boat . . . step onto the seats or the floorboard. DO NOT STEP ONTO THE SIDE OF THE BOAT." He did not call it "gunwale," its actual name, presumably because none of us would know what that was. He would "cox" this little trip—that is, serve as coxswain, which is the captain, the one who must go down with the ship—and sat himself astern, where the coxswain sits, and busied himself with coxswain business: putting the rudder into the water and affixing it to the stern, attaching yoke to rudder and untangling the yoke line. He would steer. He instructed us on protocol: identifying and setting our pins and rope rings—the fulcrum for our oars—setting our footboards, which give our bodies the needed resistance when rowing; finding and securing our oars, one to a rower. "When I give the command, 'Oars up,'" he said to us, "raise your oar vertically and set it in front of you . . . OARS UP!" We were four masts until we cast off and cleared the bulwark. "Okay," he said, "set your oars." We set out oars in their rings and pins. "ALL ROW!" We rowed. He watched us, watched the water, watched us, cajoling when necessary. "Your oar is facing the wrong way!"; "That ring is too loose—that's why your oar is slipping." He worried through the wind, which he knew was strong enough to propel the boat a knot or two in whatever direction it felt like, toward a wall, toward a shipping lane. We did not go far, looping not more than a couple of hundred yards around in the cove. But we were out there, in the cove called Hell Gate Bay, and in my imaginings subject to hydrographic forces, wind, strange destinies, various misgivings. I considered this to be my maiden voyage, thinking of maps with the name HELL GATE inscribed across this great basin, the H being about where we were now. We made it back without undue hardship.

Tuesday rows are open to everyone, but over the days that followed, I realized there was a core group to this crew: Phil and Mary Nell, and also Ismael, Katherine, Al, Joe, and a few others. All had years of experience. The Tuesday afternoon rows—community rows they are called—are not planned in advance. They don't have to be because they do not go very far. Someone in charge or someone at least knowledgeable will gauge the general situation— the direction of the current and the wind—and determine where the boat will go. Never far, maybe around the cove, maybe out to Mill Rock, or up the west channel alongside Ward's Island, almost never long out of sight of the dock. We have children aboard who are too small to row, novice rowers who eventually get the hang of rowing, or do not and do not return the next Tuesday. Occasionally someone is frightened enough to never do it again. Someone once got seasick. Someone once broke an arm. No one ever drowned, or was even thrown overboard. Most enjoy the experience, so novel in the city. In the midst of the city, but free of it, a different way of seeing.

Those early days of rowing were an assortment of anecdotes, observations, and warnings about the river, the currents, the weather, the animals recently seen. Passing near Mill Rock, Katherine told her crew that on an excursion the year before they had come upon a seal lolling about in the cove, swimming, spouting, much as humans might do in a motel pool. On another, a dolphin near the Gate. The seal was a good sign, she said, it means the water is getting cleaner; the dolphin was a bad sign, at least for the dolphin: it means he was lost.

Strangers wander into the Gate—dolphins, sometimes whales—almost always by accident, and meet their demise.

Al Stashin, another veteran crew member, says to me after some badgering, "Okay, here's a story. I was cox'ing one row . . . my crew a group of college students—big, strapping, college kids, could have been wrestlers, I don't know . . . they never rowed here, and they wanted to go up the channel. I told them the currents are against us. But they're young bucks, and of course they know better than me." Now, Al is a bear of a man, has rowed with the crew for eight or nine years, and of anyone I can imagine him taking on the currents single-handedly. "Nothing can stop them," he went on. "So I said, okay, we'll go through the Gate. We rowed into it, and as we got a little further in, they started huffing and puffing. They kept rowing, not even looking up. After watching this for a little while, I said to them, 'Look up.' They looked up and saw that they were rowing in place. All that work just to stay put."

Al tells of a rogue wave, a favorite story of his, as I have heard him repeat it to others, as well as hearing others tell it to me. "We were in the channel, near the Astoria side, not too far offshore . . . I was cox'ing and we were heading back to the davit . . . the bow oar is facing north and of course it's his job to look out for everything behind us. Okay, so he sees a wave coming, some kind of a rogue wave, a single wave . . . it's about two feet high, he says . . . and two feet is not a big wave . . . but what he meant, as we found out, is that it was two feet higher than the bow, which means it was about four feet high. That's pretty high . . . so it crashed over the bow . . . everybody got wet and the boat took on a lot of water. So there we were, getting lower in the water, bailing like crazy . . . but it was a mystery . . . where the wave came from . . . there was no other wave before or after, it came and went through . . . we never found out what it was, where it came from . . . maybe a sudden discharge from one of the outflow pipes."

Maybe so. There are plenty of outflow pipes along the East River that empty overflow that collects on land from heavy rain. But that would have been some surge. After hearing Al's story, I was immediately on the lookout for a rogue wave; I saw none, but kept in mind the possibility. It's strange to think of waves on the East River, but they happen, and each one has energy, and energy gives meaning: a wave can rock you or lull you to sleep—or over-turn you. The East River is not the open sea but its connection to it causes some of its oddities. Most waves are not waves generated by wind, nor the rolls from shallow coastal waters. Most are generated by river traffic, wakes coming off the tug and barge units and the tanker barges that routinely pass through. When fully loaded and low in the water, their massive bulk and weight sends a wake of long and deep-set waves across the river's surface. Rowers keep an eye to ships for two reasons: one, to keep their fragile hulls out of harm's way, and two, to ready it for the wake that will eventually cross the boat. We get ready by pointing the boat at a 45-degree angle to the incoming wake. If straight-on to the wake, you risk being washed over; if abeam, or parallel, you risk being flipped. The oddity is the rebound. The East River channels, being as nar-row as they are and lined with stalwart bunkers of concrete or rip-rap, will cause an incoming wave to rebound and head back out to the river. If close enough to the shore walls, it is possible to get caught in both simultaneously. But farther out in the channel, the risk is that the ship has long passed and is out of your thinking by the time the rebound hits you—as though from nowhere. Here on the water is a promise of such oddities. Also, the welcome of a new vocabulary, remnants of forgotten histories: gunwale (pronounced "gunnel"), the top of the boat's sidewall, where guns were placed when boats had guns; "coxswain" (pronounced "cox'n"), the boat's steerer and in our case also the captain. On a boat, teamwork is a necessity and not an empty plati-tude. Rules are followed. When on a boat you take the water seriously, lest it throw you, which it will try to do, always. Stable ground is unseen below water. Bottom becomes the most meaningful word in your vocabulary. It is no wonder sailors are a superstitious lot. In the floating world, you feel nearly weightless, but not free.

The Open Boats

The boats we use are Whitehall gigs, a design after the old working boats of New York harbor, when they were used as tenders between anchored ships and docks. The Crew owned and had built two: the St. David's and the Eight-Plus, each about twenty-five feet long with a beam of about four feet. For any excursion, each boat has a coxswain and a crew. The coxswain steers, tugging on a rope to swing the rudder left or right. As I've said, the coxswain is the captain, responsible for all that goes on, and is the only one to face forward. A crew on a given row numbers anywhere from four to seven. Since there are four seats and four oars, if there are more than four rowers, some must double up on the seats and take turns rowing. Rowing is done backward: that is, rowers sit with their backs to the direction of the boat's movement. The seats in the middle are sometimes called "engine rooms," and Mary Nell tells us the rowers are called "engines." The rowers at stern and bow are called metonymically: "stroke oar" and "bow oar." The stroke oar sits in front, facing the cox, setting the pace for the other oars to follow. The bow oar is at the bow of the boat, behind and elevated slightly above the others. It is the bow's responsibility to pass word onto the cox of happenings on the water, such as other boats and ships advancing from the rear, and also to hoist the bow flag and to receive and toss the bow lines. Oars alternate: the first and third on the starboard side, the second and fourth on the port side. The stroke and the bow oars are different in length and weight and both are different still from the two middle oars, which are alike to each other. The two middle oars have no specialty, other than being engines. Often the middle is where new rowers sit.

Conditions vary for each excursion: the exact combination of tide, weather, currents, and wind never repeats. A cloud bank appears over the city on the west, a potential threat. A quick check of the weather on a smart phone: "Nope," says Al, "it's moving to the north, past us." Rain itself is not a threat; getting wet after all is part of the adventure. In a light rain, being in the water is a strange and calming experience, especially if there is no wind. Joe muses about the rain—that it seems to "flatten" the water, calming it. Lightning is another story. The sky darkens, and the air suddenly stills itself. No wind means no rippling water (Lesson 1: The wind causes the water to ripple, not the currents). The water is glassy, and under such conditions we seem to slow down, take the river on its own terms, which are now easy and free under the dark clouds of a summer afternoon. When we see a bolt of lightning, we turn and start back for the dock. But slowly. A second bolt speeds us up. It doesn't matter if the bolts are miles away (Lesson 2: The sky is wide, and in an open boat your head is the highest thing around).

Tuesday afternoon rows are short and local, maybe around Mill Rock, maybe a quick loop within Hell Gate Basin, especially on very windy days, or a short jaunt up the Harlem River (where the currents are rarely severe) to Little Hell Gate. Names of places are localized: Little Hell Gate is the "cove." Conversation during these brief excursions is idle talk of quotidian things, often of things of the water, found or seen, the passing around of information, differences in conditions between today and the other day. Whenever it comes to the character of the water, all eyes and ears are open:

"The buoy is gone" (a buoy had been spotted days ago and now has disappeared).

"Currents are ebbing here, but over there . . ."

"Barge coming up on stern . . ."

"Did you see the boat upended in the water a few days ago?" "No—where?" "It's gone now."

We use a strange combination of nautical parlance and city speak: "The tide is ebbing, on its way downtown . . ."

"What's that?" A giant cube appears to be floating upstream by itself, no tug in sight. Impossible, we know, but what is the explanation . . . where is the tug? We hold back . . . and then pull around to find a small tug on the far side of the barge, the barge perfectly obscuring its tug.

In a boat with a low freeboard, you no longer look down at the water but across it. I dip my hand into the water and lift it to my mouth, fingers to mouth, fear of oils, taste of salt. Being at the surface one appreciates how water in action is *not* flat, that it undulates and whirls, has shape, is capped with swells. I see a sinewy line drawn across the water, crossing in front of the bow and extending several yards distant off starboard, something that looks like a trail of soap suds. "Joe, does this have to do with the currents?" I was guessing, but Joe was the most knowledgeable of the crew about the currents, and it is to him that the crew will often go with questions. "Yes, I call them current fences." We crossed it, and the boat suddenly swung 90 degrees to port. "See?" said Joe, almost as if the river decided to demonstrate. "*I* call them current fences . . . they're like eddy fences." Current fences, his term; eddy fences, a dictionary term: the edge of an eddy in the calmer water surrounding it. Pass through a current fence or an eddy fence, and it will change your direction because your boat straddles the fence, an untenable position. Current fences demark neighboring streams of current. Their patterns and length change minute to minute, appear and disappear, extend themselves in different directions, breaking up or rejoining. Out here, there is no predictable order of things. A quick sputter, unnerving for its suddenness, a small demonstration of capriciousness. "When there were rocks here, it must have been worse," I said. "They don't call it Hell Gate for nothing," said Joe. We do nothing to recover, the river sets us right (Lesson 3: We are here at the mercy of the river, and it can do anything).

On a Tuesday afternoon row, in the seat in front of me sit a woman and her young son. "Do you know what this place is?" she asks him as we pull near Mill Rock. She gives him a hint: "We see it from our living room window." He still doesn't answer. "Bird Island," she says. Good name for it, I think; after all, it is a bird sanctuary of sorts, not officially sanctioned, but in actuality: a place the birds know they can come without being bothered. The Parks Department does not allow human beings here, though boats pull into the cove to get out of the currents or rest a spell. On this evening it is crowded with gulls and cormorants. All kinds of birds are said to transit here, alighting from their fly-bys on the North Atlantic flyway. Cormorants, dark and smoky-gray feathered, are today the largest segment of the population. They could not be seen nor heard from shore but are now very visible and very much within earshot. The cormorants are reclusive creatures. I have never seen one fly over land, unlike gulls, which swoop through the city skies, sharing ownership with pigeons, hawks, sparrows, and crows. Here the cormorants stay to themselves, thousands of them, filling the air with their noisy raucous voices. "Bird Island" is said to be the most common name in the world for an island.

We decide one day to cross the river to Hallett's Point, the tide changes leaving us no time to go anywhere far. Phil is the cox, and also the teacher. The rest of us are now "intermediates," having some experience but not much. We might also learn something about boat handling, as good a time as any as it is a dark day of clouds and wind. There will be object lessons. As we move downriver, we see a cluster of small boats and what appear to be small logs or river crap. They are swimmers. You need to be aware of the situation at all times, Phil has said: "situational awareness." And now the situation is Swim Around Manhattan Day, in which swimmers do their version of a marathon by swimming a complete circuit around Manhattan Island. At this moment about a dozen swimmers are in our vicinity, their bodies mostly submerged; they are all bathing cap and spandex, the color of the water, and barely breaking the choppy surface. Each swimmer is accompanied by a small boat or kayak, friends presumably, enlisted as support in case the swimmer tires. "One thing you learn is that you cannot stay still," says Phil. "If you stop rowing, you still move." We row away from a cluster of swimmers and kayaks and toward another. We stop, but the current sets us hard toward a seawall. We push out and find an opening between some swimmers. We continue across the river, "vectoring," a strategy Phil teaches us, the idea being to cut the current at a 45-degree angle and head for a spot below where we expect to land on the side opposite, and then let the current help. The swimmers are behind us; ships are in the distance, but we are safe. We round Hallett's Point, which puts us in Pot Cove. The crown of what is left of Pot Rock is below, out of sight. Nothing remaining of the *HMS Hussar*, either. Too bad.

Tuesday rows are open to everyone. Saturday rows are not. Help out with the boats on Tuesdays, wheel them to and from their storage container to the davit, stick around to clean them after each row, look like you're interested, and you might be invited to a Saturday row. One Tuesday evening, I catch Phil and Ismael looking at me as though choosing up sides for a baseball game. I hear Phil say to Ismael: "He'll go." Phil says to me, "You want to go through Hell Gate?" ("Psst ... hey, kid ...") The grown-up in me nods yes. "Yes, I do. That's why I'm here."

CHAPTER 7

From Swerve of Shore to Bend of Bay

The Gate

To ride through Hell Gate in an open boat . . .

To see what Adriaen Block saw . . .

To listen for Danckaert's whistling, or Denton's hideous roaring, to see if his Charon is on call . . .

Or,

To emulate Poe in his skiff, rowing around Blackwell's Island . . .

A Voyage of Discovery and Exploration

I am by no means a mariner. But no sooner do I step into a boat than my imagination gives in to all sorts of marine fancy, in no special order: *the Pequod . . . the Seven Seas . . . the Nina, the Pinta, the Santa Maria . . . the curraghs of St. Brendan . . . the Ancient Mariner . . . islands . . . windward, leeward . . . the white whale . . . sharks . . . Captain Ahab . . . Captain Nemo . . . the long tentacles of squid . . . improbable sea monsters . . . black skies . . . drowning.* Where knowledge is lacking, one indulges in atavistic fable and myth.

The float plan was simple: a circumnavigation of Ward's/Randall's Island—from the davit east across Hell Gate Basin, up through the Gate and on to the Brothers, and a return through the Bronx Kill and the lower Harlem, a short odyssey of nearly certain outcome: a safe return home. The crew had circled this route before. For them, it was a minor trip, a run around the block, a way to stay limber, or a place to go when time and tide was not right for longer excursions. Hell Gate offered no special thrill for them who did this all the time; for me, it was a venture into the center of a world I had explored only from its edges. One other thing the crew had in common: they knew the name of the place. Hell Gate, not Hell's Kitchen, not High Gate, not any of the other names I have overheard.

I was not involved in the planning of this excursion—but I do like to know where I'm going. So I went to the nautical charts, for aesthetic pleasure as much as knowledge: to get an alternate view of city topography. Charts invert the world as we know it, a counterpoint to maps. Maps detail the land and leave the water as empty spaces of blue. Nautical charts reverse the emphasis: the land is barely charted—streets near the water are drawn and some are labeled; what buildings are labeled are those that are famous (the Empire State Building) or else those that mariners might use to keep themselves oriented. Streets end only a short distance inland; some buildings are situated and marked but not named—"hospital," not "Metropolitan Hospital." The water, on the other hand, is jammed with more markings and abbreviated language than you would ever imagine from a walk along a riverbank. Hydrographic lines, depth soundings every few square yards, and the river bottom is categorized: "G" (gravel), "Rky" (rocks), "obtsns," "ruins," "wks" (wrecks) for underwater impediments. Old piers are noted (the dilapidated and rotting as "ruins"); buoys and locations of pipes and cables are marked in dashed lines; bridge heights and spans between piers are depicted; long straight lines denote channels, small juts of land, and outcroppings you didn't know existed from a map because they don't matter—strange codes full of meaning, everything a ship must know. At Hell Gate, NOAA Chart No. 12339 shows several "obtsns," rocks, even a few "wks," and is of course crowded with channel depths. At Bronx Kill, a mudflat spreads across its eastern mouth. And even the old names that one might think extinct are very much present on No. 12339: Rhinelanders Reef, Hallett's Point, Pot Cove, the Hog Back, Negro Point, Ways Reef—included not out of nostalgia but because these places could still wrack a steel hull.

Rowboats, with a draft of only a couple of feet, have no such worry. But legwork and personal surveys are useful. No matter how elaborate the chart detail is, it is static, and actual conditions might not match the stated descriptions. Water means change. Days before, Al and Ismael scouted the Bronx

Kill—the only questionable part of the excursion. Land accumulation has pushed both sides of what was once another raucous Hell Gate channel ever closer to each other, close enough so that a ballplayer on the Randall's side can have an easy catch with a warehouse worker on the Bronx side. Al and Ismael eyed the area for subtle shifts in topography: any new hazards, constructions, or destructions? Had the mudflats spread? Was the Kill now choked with mud and garbage? If we misjudged the tide, the Kill would be too shallow to row through, and we would have to either "punt," to crawl along using our oars as legs, or else, if grounding ourselves, get out and carry the boat, like the old explorers who had to portage between two streams.

It was a perfect day for a row: water high, weather fair, and wind from the south and combined with a tide in flood stage would give us good propulsion through the Gate. We made a late start, which would later alter our float plan. We pushed across the bay until we passed the northern tip of Mill Rock, and then came in closer to Ward's Island. Slow current here, and quick, spiky chops on the water, not unlike what you might see when piranha are feeding just below. We neared the Hog Back, where the chops picked up, almost to whitewater. As we were turning at Negro Point at the southeast corner of Ward's Island, the current picked up. So did the noise of the water. *This is the Gate*, I announced to myself to mark the moment, the real thing, the water agitated but not dangerous, whitewater, but no river slop splashing into our faces. I became aware of a low, thunderous din. I thought of Denton's hideous roaring, but it was not that: it was the stream of traffic on the Triborough Bridge overhead echoing downward and between the bluffs on either side of the channel. The boat bounced through the whitewater, but we maintained our oars and our pace. On both sides of the channel are trees, brush, green. Adriaen Block's channel, the *Hel-gutt*, the opening, a way toward something. Perhaps it was the sound of rushing water that reminded Block of home. A couple of minutes and we were through the rough part, past the Triborough and past the Hell Gate Railroad Bridge, coming alongside the industrial flank of Ward's Island. The wastewater treatment plant, a DPA vessel tied to the dock. It shouldn't take more than a few minutes to be all the way through, past the Bronx Kill, and at the Brothers.

To be a rower is to be a thinker and a planner, not only at the start but throughout the voyage. Assessing the lateness of our arrival by the time we reached the Kill, Ismael decided to forego our continuing on to the Brothers. Too far upriver, though we were close enough to make out its brambles and the brickwork of the old Riverside Hospital. Well, we might have made it, but we would be taking a chance going back through the Kill. Its water level might be too low by the time we got back, and we'd have to punt. No one wanted to punt. So we turned into the Kill earlier than planned.

The Kill is narrow, hidden, silent, in contrast to the Gate, which is open, noisy, and boisterous. Placid, gentle, barely there anymore. Before the land-fill, the Kill was much wider, much less defined. Never very deep all the way through, it was hardly navigable except by light-draft flatboat or rowboat. Its currents were stronger, its edges lush, like Little Hell Gate to the south. Now, another rarely trodden nook, a thin salt marsh being restored, the work of the Randall's Island Park Alliance, the same group that cleaned up the junk and developed the one at Little Hell Gate. On another excursion, on foot, I had met up with one of their naturalists, Christopher Girgenti. There are actually two marshes, he told me, one on each bank. The side we were on, Randall's Island, was the one RIPA had been tending. But on the other side, he said, "notice the cordgrass . . . that's the result of seeds floating from here to there." "Spatina," he went on, "is the bed of the marsh," growing very quickly, blaz-ing brilliant colors in September, then dying and settling in to become a root mat. We watched as something shadowy flew between us and the descend-ing sun: a barn swallow, if I remember correctly, looking for food. Another close behind. After a couple of loops around, and not seeing anything worth their time, they flew off to the next stop on the Flyway: probably Jamaica Bay, said Christopher. He was good at this, could easily spot a flying thing, and where I would say "bird," he would say, "barn swallow," or "yellow-crowned nighthawk," or "herring gull." Looking out from what used to be the Sunken Meadow sand spit and was now a set of manicured ballfields, he said, "Bright Passage." "Yeah," I said—and thought, this is how images stick and errors in interpretation compound themselves. But this view, all the way past Rikers and LaGuardia, out to the Whitestone Bridge, on a bright day, it *was* a bright passage.

And it was also bright at this moment, as our Whitehall gig cruised through. We took down the flags so they would not get clipped by the low bridge ahead. Unnecessary, it turned out: plenty of head room, shadowy inside. Its narrowness and quietness was odd, maybe unnerving, shallow, calm, no visible human presence on either shore, the kind of place in an old movie just before the native villagers pop up from behind the brush or an alligator slips off the bank. Therese asks our location, and someone points: Randall's Island this side, the Bronx that side. She looks amused: "Everything looks different from the water." We glided through easily, a calm stream, dark, shallow. Ismael pointed out a beaver dam. "A what?" "Well, that's what I call it," he said. Someone had laid boulders and chunks of old rip-rap across the stream, a kind of causeway. Never completed, but at low water exposed enough to allow crossing. Soon we were through, the mouth widening. To port: the NYPD marina, where police boats are fueled and maintained. In front, the lift span of the Triborough Bridge, between Randall's Island and Manhattan. Manhattan: from the Gate, the Kill, back to the city. We turned into the deeper water of the Harlem, headed downriver, past the fishing pier at 107th Street, under the footbridge at 103rd, into Hell Gate Bay, and back to the davit at 96th.

I took stock: turbulence and an idyll in a single afternoon. Hell Gate, rollicking but hardly a threat to the "well acquainted," a far cry from the *Helgutt*. I had achieved my immediate ambition: I had passed through the vortex around which spirals the city of New York, and had come away clean. In *Moby Dick*, Ishmael ponders the nature of voyages, how at their most prosaic, circumnavigations merely lead back to their starting point. But voyages may also lead to discoveries "sweet and strange," or in the pursuit of phantoms, might also lead to "barren mazes." Our excursions on the East River always returned to the davit whence we started, and for me at least brought to the fore a maze of old questions: Where, or what, is this *Hellegat*?

From the Gate Southwest (Red Hook)

Ambition achieved, it was time to extend ambition. Besides, rowing was becoming an alternate way of seeing, a new way of deliberate movement through a city where all things seemed to hurtle away from the center. The more time I spent in a boat, the less susceptible I became to nautical fantasy. I might, as well, be able to chase this name *Hellegat* through the entire stretch that Adriaen Block had named. I volunteered for more excursions—the "long rows"—and there are only two directions on the East River: below Hell Gate and above Hell Gate, southwest or east. Marine radio callers on the East River use south and east, reserving north and south for the Hudson River on the other side of Manhattan.

The first long row was southwest to Red Hook. Red Hook: about eight miles south of the davit at Hell Gate Bay; in Brooklyn; a waterfront neighborhood old enough to have a Dutch name—*Roode Hoek*—for its red-clay soil and the jut into the East River it used to be—tree-canopied, narrow-laned, with a shorefront of bricked Civil War–era warehouses, home of the Atlantic Basin, and now using its industrial/archaeological tracings to bootstrap itself into contemporary hipness with lobster huts and artist communes. Also, they have a giant IKEA store, and this is one of the things we look forward to— IKEA's famous Swedish meatballs. There is talk of doing some shopping. This is not exactly going to be a working cruise.

This downtown stretch of the East River is citified, for the most part bulwarked by concrete walls and stout rip-rap, edges as well defined as a canal. What industrial past Manhattan once had along here is now obliterated by apartment buildings and high-rises, hospitals, the UN, the FDR, and a few small parks pocketed at the dead ends of streets. The old bluffs along the river above the Queensborough Bridge, the ones Poe saw and wrote about, still exist, hemmed in by walls of massive stone blocks, weathered and brown. The thin strip now occupied by the FDR used to be a street, called at different times Marginal Street and Exterior Street, hidden and isolated by virtue of the bluffs. No crosstown streets intersected here because any point of intersection would be a vertical drop of thirty feet or more. All streets therefore dead-ended at the top of the bluff, which was the end of the world for those who marked their lives in slow steady footsteps.

We checked out the boats, dropped them into the water by means of the creaky davit, and headed out, late as usual, crossing Hell Gate Basin east to get to Hallett's Cove, where we would enter the channel on the other side of Roosevelt Island and head southwest, Long Island City on our port side to the east. To our starboard side is the lighthouse, its fishermen stationed along the island's prow. The industrial past of the Queens waterfront is in crumbling evidence: old piers of rotting piles, sandy strips, an art park: the Socrates Sculpture Garden, where artists work in public, welding steel beams into abstract sculptures or otherwise engaged with electric tools, their work barely distinguishable from the objects rusting beside tall grasses and weed beds.

Fixed in the channel are three buoys in single file, or what look like buoys. Actually, as Al explains, they are turbines, powered by the speed of the water, generating enough energy to assist in the illumination of a parking garage on Roosevelt Island. The current builds on one side, and small whirlpools take shape on the down-current side, a model of what the rocks and ledges once did. But the rush of the water creates an illusion of motion on the part of the turbines themselves, that these fixed objects are the things that appear to be moving through the water. We pass under a bridge, the only one that connects Roosevelt Island to Queens; the more famous Queensborough Bridge spans and shadows the island but has no off-ramp for traffic.

Below Roosevelt Island, the river opens up. Off the southern tip, another collection of rocks, Belmont Island, created from the detritus of railroad tunnels dug under the East River. Famous landmarks surround us: the glass-sheathed Secretariat Building of the United Nations, and on the Long Island City side, the giant Pepsi-Cola sign. Also inlets and more inlets, some unused piers, others refurbished into ferry slips. We keep an eye out: "That ferry down there," Al says, pointing to a Long Island City slip, "is coming this way." He does a quick mental calculation of its speed and distance, and of our speed and nearness to the ferry dock: "We'd better haul ass." We made it with room to spare, but this brief episode points to the danger of traffic down here. Even in water, the East River, the movement of ships and boats and its aftermath. The river is a road down here: busy. And wide. Thus the wakes from passing ships take longer to get to you; and since we are near the middle of the river, the echoes of the wakes off the walls take even longer, but they will reach you.

Gantry State Park, on the Long Island City side of the river, is typical of the new waterfront: a reshaping from heavy metal to light. Two gantries sit side by side at the water's edge—thus the name. They were built to lift railroad cars from barges coming across the river from Manhattan onto rails eventually fanning throughout Long Island. Separated from their original purpose, the gantries exist now as a nod to the neighborhood's muscular past, emblems of defunct industry. Short stretches of rail have been left in their original state, practically disappearing amid new grasses and new stonework. New age as pale reflection. Shiny steel guardrails along the piers' edges, the occasional fisherman tossing a line, small signs telling those who fish what they can and cannot do, can and cannot catch. Newly developed residential towers of glass, cheaper than Manhattan's when built but now giving Manhattan a run for its money, towering glass walls lining streets emptied of crowds and life. I had come across Gantry Park on earlier walks around Long Island City, in particular a narrow strip of a park that ran the length of one block. Seemed an odd location and shape for a park. It was not until I got to the river and saw the gantries with their tracks that I realized this strip was the right of way for the railroad that once came through. Tracks on the other side of 11th Street lead to the Hunter's Point railyard, still in use, and these lead to Sunnyside Yard, still in use, some tracks of which coalesce into the two tracks that circle north and back to the East River and cross it at Hell Gate, bound for New England. All of these pieces are part of a greater scheme.

Further below Gantry Park is Newtown Creek, the watery border separating Queens from Brooklyn that empties into the East River down here, its wide weedy mouth completely uninviting: "drab and oily . . . more tonnage carried here than on the Mississippi"—comments written decades ago in the *WPA Guide*, sounding more civic boast than alarm. And yet even here are efforts to make Long Island City and the East River look virginal again: riverbanks with new plantings, a fresh conservation area. We pass the Domino Sugar refinery. Sugar refining was once a major industry in New York, but no more. This Domino factory is out of business, its exterior festooned with the work of graffiti writers, monumental lettering and cartoonish artwork befitting the hugeness of the complex—and quite possibly the future location of more unaffordable housing for those who like living on the river. Still further is the Brooklyn Navy Yard, once the builder of warships, and the burial place for prison ships from the American Revolution, bones under muck. There are names to distract me: Wallabout Bay, once a wide arm of the river, now yet another swamp, named for its early French Walloon settlers.

A few aspects of the downtown section of the East River are noteworthy. One is the set of bridges: the Williamsburg Bridge, the Jew's Highway, for the thousands who crossed the river from the lower east side to what were then the clean and broad streets of Brooklyn; the Manhattan Bridge, handsome and utilitarian, which means uncelebrated . . . the Brooklyn, the first to span the river and the most celebrated bridge in the universe of Greater New York: Hart Crane's symbol of America, O Harp and Altar. This part of the East River was New York's earliest port. It was less wide than the Hudson on the other side of Manhattan, and its constant motion prevented freezing except in the most frigid weather. The Dutch built and rebuilt wharves along Manhattan's shoreline; they collected garbage and useless litter of home and workplace and used it to extend land outward into the water and build wharves, a process continued by the English, and then the Americans, grist for future core samples, time capsules of the city's continuum.

Someone asks, "How deep is it here?" Perhaps fifty feet under us, and over there, one hundred feet . . . nautical charts show a variation . . . if the river were drained what would it show? Rocks, pinnacles, hulks of iron and steel ships, maybe some worm-holed timber of old wooden ships preserved in mud. Down here, as we near Governors Island, we row through traffic and bounce over the wakes and their echoes off the bulwarks. Splashing. Sloshing. We are well aware of the received notions of filth and river scum, but the East River, constantly on the move between Sound and harbor presents no danger from poisons, as long as we keep our mouths shut. There is a lot of traffic at the moment. Experienced small boat operators, when speaking of the difficulties of this river, will point to the obstructions and the currents, but more so to the traffic. We stay aside the ship channel, hugging the Brooklyn shore. We pass through Buttermilk Channel, Governors Island on our starboard, the Atlantic Basin on our port. Governors Island—Nutten Island to the Dutch for all the nut trees—was once a large island that eventually eroded into a smaller one and was subsequently built up again when they dug the Lexington Avenue subway. The dirt went to the southern end of the island. Long ago, Buttermilk Channel was shallow. The gardener of the then governor (about 1750) supposedly was able to propel himself across in a canoe without a paddle simply by pushing himself with his foot. As the port of New York grew by landfill and wharves constricting the East River, the channel was gouged by the accelerating water, deepening the channel enough to accommodate vessels larger than canoes, foot power no longer an option.

Around the corner, the actual "red hook," we make it at last to the beach at Valentino Park. We debark and haul the boats up the beach. Too intent on debarking, we make an error regarding the tide that won't bite us for another hour or so. Nearby, some kayakers have also put in and are resting on the beach. One doesn't think often of beaches on city rivers, but years of disuse and abandonment will ultimately erode the works of man and replace them with sand. Most are small spits, foul, muddy, pocked with stones and debris. But on this afternoon, Valentino Park is clean. One can imagine the narrow spit as a turn to the sea. We break, go our separate ways. Some head for IKEA, others just free themselves to stretch and walk, regain their land legs. I buy a hot dog from a nearby vendor. Red Hook is noted for its food vendors, key lime pie, lobster rolls, sold out of small carts run by young entrepreneurs, or else hole-in-the- wall, ramshackle operations, clean but with the pride of the hip dive. Behind them are the Civil War–era warehouses now converted to workshops for artists, crafts people, long brick buildings of three stories with small, dark windows and wood clapboard shutters. It is one of the virtues of neighborhoods to be downtrodden enough so that the city forgets them and doesn't bother with the expense of condemnation and demolition. Later, when taste changes and fashion brings the abandoned back into style, no one wants to tear anything down. Being fashionable, I once considered living here, but as convenient Red Hook is by boat, it is damn inconvenient by subway.

Its name for the red soil indicated the activity most important in the area at the time: farming. Later on, fishing became another industry. With the coming of the Erie Canal in 1825, Red Hook prospered along with New York, becoming an offloading port for freight from the nation's interior. The Erie Basin, the Atlantic Basin—harbors within harbors, facilities for shipping and ship building and maintenance. It was a working-class area, and retains a sinister look, skeevy, the floes of urban myth: rats within and without, cement shoes, the cannonball splash. And location: the only point of land where the face of the Statue of Liberty is viewable dead on—the putative locus of *On the Waterfront*, book and movie, and all the Marlon Brandos who have come and gone in the meantime. I'd been through here before, walking the streets, on a hunt for lobster rolls and key lime pie. I felt like the innocent lug in Thomas Wolfe's story "Only the Dead Know Brooklyn," who wandered through Brooklyn, map in hand, exploring neighborhoods whose names intrigued him—Canarsie, Bensonhoist, East Noo Yawk—and Red Hook.

After spending some time walking around, without a map but an awareness of streets, I return to the boat, and meet up with the error of our earlier haste. The tide is coming in slowly but noticeably, the water invading higher on the sand, a small wavelet strong enough to lift the stern of the boat off the sand and set it back down. Successive waves begin to lift the stern in increasing frequency, and soon, the whole boat begins to bob and toss. Two-foot-high wakes that arrive on shore from passing barges and oilers only add to our woes. Katherine gamely descends deeper and deeper into the water to attempt to push the boats up. At the bow I try to pull the bow through dead sand. In vain. The kayakers see our troubles, our boat now being battered about like a bath toy, and leap up to lend a hand, pulling the vessel farther up the beach.

Then comes the rain. It lasts but a few minutes, a quick tropical storm from the south, but is strong enough to drench us before it moves north, leaving as fast as it came. Eventually, everyone returns from their respective jaunts. We embark, shove off for home, the harbor now calm, a radiant sky with a sun breaking from behind clouds, rays cast to earth. But something is not right, something eerie about the long scene across sky and harbor, and I realize no ships are in sight. No ferries, no boats of any kind. There is no sound, as though while we were away, all who had lived here in the city suddenly upped and left. The tide being with us, we do not row, merely drift upriver, using our oars and yoke line only to steer and keep the boat on something of a course, in the channel, away from running up against stunted piles or aground onto deceptive shallows.

We drift back the way we came, and in the distance, past Roosevelt Island, the familiar sight of Hell Gate comes into view. The water beneath us begins to churn, or rather we have returned to the place where it always churns. We take up our oars again, necessary now to cross the basin to the davit. We are good and strong, a single unit. The most exquisite sight in rowing is when all four oars are in synch with one another. There is, I learn from Mary Nell, a musical term for this, denoting rhythm and concert: "swing." When all oars are in synch, the boat is said to be in "swing." (The opposite condition, when all oars are flailing about, is called appropriately, the "drowning spider.") Steve and I are in perfect swing, our oars hitting the surface of the water at the same moment and our oar blades describing the same arc, as though they are both attached to a pantograph. It is an equally exquisite sound, the swoosh of an oar blade hitting the water times four: a harmony of swoosh in quadruplex. "Blind people make the best rowers," says Mary Nell, not quite facetiously, "they know how to listen." Back on shore, I mention our synchronicity to Steve. He says, "Not many people can keep up with me." Steve was one of our strongest rowers, and his remark was meant as a compliment, but then I remembered I was the stroke oar on that occasion, and he should have been following me. Steve was also among the most individual of rowers.

On another afternoon, we head out on a short excursion downriver, a circumnavigation of Roosevelt Island, all we have time for given the direction and timing of the currents. Ismael is cox. We begin from the same starting point—the davit across Hell Gate Basin—and this time head down the west channel of the river, between Roosevelt Island and Manhattan. Roosevelt is a name I am still unaccustomed to, having known it long ago as Welfare (institutional history codified), and from my reading as Blackwell's. Roosevelt is completely circled by pedestrian paths and narrow asphalt roads, with little traffic other than cyclists and walkers. Parallel to Manhattan, Roosevelt can be measured as Manhattan is measured, in blocks: about thirty-nine, from 86th to 47th Streets.

We row past the lighthouse, past the tiers of the FDR and John Finley Walk, alongside the bluffs. We pass underneath the Queensborough Bridge and continue past Roosevelt Island, past Belmont Island, where we turn around. The current has not yet turned to flood, so we have some time on our hands. It is late afternoon, and the river is now entirely in shadow from the buildings of Manhattan. We open ourselves to side investigations and coasting, exploring inlets. One inlet is adjacent to a monstrous Long Island City building, one of those new high-rises with views of Manhattan, at less than (advertised) Manhattan prices. The building appears to be empty. We count interior lights: one, two . . . maybe six in a building of twenty stories or more. "It's not quite dark yet," says Al. "Or maybe no one lives here," says I. We putter around. Something is floating several yards off. Ismael picks up his paddle—the paddle used by coxswains for control—and paddles the boat over. A soccer ball, the result we guess of an errant kick somewhere along the riverbank. He reaches for it with his paddle and hauls it in, a transparent film of oily water and river gook clinging to its surface. "No, I don't want it in the boat." He tosses it back into the water. Harmful infectious substances—he is thinking, we all are thinking, of the integrity of the ship.

Not far from the inlet, just opposite the southern tip of Roosevelt Island, still on the Long Island City side, we notice lights, hear music, a pier-side attraction. We want to investigate, so we pull a little closer, and when we see a dock in good shape—with solid foundations and what appear to be strong dock cleats—we let that decide for us. Soft city: a spacious patio, picnic tables, awnings, people milling about. Talk, music, paper plates, bathrooms. Climbing to the dock is not an easy task, as there are no ladders; evidently it is not a well-used dock, at least not for Whitehall gigs. As we climb, a few children gather haltingly, looking upon us as if we are aliens come from the dark. Their parents do not shield them, so they know we can't be too dangerous: mere curiosities. I think of the place as an outpost, an island in the midst of a dark sea, dark on all sides, water and the interior of Long Island City: here, we can get a beer or two with our hot dogs. Such side ventures are not often attempted by the crew, but Ismael knows we have a little time for an escapade. Apt to be captain in the sense of being an independent entity, master of his own ship, disciplined in terms of work and procedure, but nevertheless alone in the sea, far from meddling superiors, and therefore the decider of all things aboard ship. A little side trip won't hurt. Nevertheless, we are all engines on this boat, so none of us get drunk.

We linger no longer than an hour or so, listening to the music, making light talk and jokes, enjoying the night. Finally, replenished and relieved, we get back to the boat. Children see us off, but not too closely. One of the crew waves, and some wave back; most are expressionless. Once back in the boat, I realize that though I had peeked inland and down the dark streets, I had not bothered to look for any signs of where we were. I did not even get the name of our little snack bar. To this day, I can give directions only from the water.

We stayed away long enough for late dusk to turn into dark night. A passing boat with a white light gives Ismael a teaching moment: What are the rules of the road? What do the lights mean? Red lights, green lights? White lights? Small boats must carry lights at night so they can be seen—this is one of the rules of boating. But I think of Captain Brucato at the helm of one of his tugs and what he says about the small lights on a small boat in the middle of a broad river: "another bouncing glittering light lost in the city's skyline."

From the Gate Northeast (Whitestone)

The medieval Irish have a word, *immram*, for a genre of sea tales written by the monks and adventurers who crossed the North Atlantic: to Iceland, where Brendan thought he discovered the gates of Hell, and beyond, possibly to North America. Literally, *immram* means "oaring or rowing around," and taking the word literally, casually, it describes exactly what we do: oaring around, rowing here, rowing there, across Hell Gate basin, memory of rocks, cacophony of water, into the Gate. Despite our careful planning, there is a kind of aimlessness to our activity. For one thing, we are not merchantmen and not fishermen who need to set out to work; our expeditions are discretionary, recreational. In our case, we go to do what there is to do: explore, work our muscles, beat the summer heat, listen to the slosh of oar through water. There is no need to set out, but if we do, we have to get back.

We planned a row this time to the north and east of Hell Gate, toward Throgs Neck, where the East River comes to its end and Long Island Sound begins—not source, not mouth, but a line accepted locally as geographic convention. At least I was hoping we could target Throgs Neck, so as to record a complete physical unit of work to my marine excursions—that is, to have rowed from one end of the East River strait (Red Hook) to the other. But alas: "No way we will make Throgs Neck—and back," says Phil. It is that "and back" that separates the thinker from the Sunday sailor, the pause preceding it to emphasize the point. So we set our sights on Whitestone, a Queens neighborhood on a jut of Long Island's North Shore between the Bronx-Whitestone

Bridge and the Throgs Neck Bridge. Phil knew of a beach here, in Francis Lewis Park, just east of the Bronx-Whitestone. It was much like the beach at Red Hook, only longer, wider, and like most East River beaches, a mix of grayish sand, native rock, and junk concrete, rebar rods rusted and exposed. The park is named after the Long Island Revolutionary hero Francis Lewis, who maintained a home here and whose name is also applied to a nearby boulevard. Phil had scouted the neighborhood the week before, by car. He reported: "The park has water fountains and bathrooms, but no food . . . 14th Avenue has delis and pizza places, but it's several blocks away." Obviously, he was reluctant to let us roam too freely lest we lose our sense of time and delay our return, or make it impossible until the next favorable current twelve hours later. "So pack your own food . . . along with water, of course, sunscreen, hats, and whatever else." Like camp. Personal preparation always includes water, sandwiches, sunblock, a hat, notebook and pens, and for me, since I am something of a bleeder, band aids. A small pack is fine by me; in fact, I like the idea of carrying all my worldly possessions in a satchel I can carry on my back—what does not fit is dross.

Whitestone: more suburban than urban, shoreline more open than walled, more river and sky than city, about six miles from the davit at 96th Street. I had little experience with the river up here, an occasional boat ride, a few strolls through parks, a few walks along shoreline paths. From maps, I picked up a good idea of the geography: an arm of the East River much different than the one below Hell Gate, where the river is defined crisply, lined with bulwarks. Up here, the river opens up, and is set on both sides with inlets cut deeply into the shoreline, coves wide or narrow, bays of wide muddy flats, and the outlets of small streams, not so much different in my imaginings than the Hellegat. The Bronx River opens into a wide mouth here, as does Westchester Creek a mile or so to the east, and across is the Flushing River (or Creek) from Queens. None of these is navigable for an appreciable length by any but the smallest boats; all meander, all are dirty, none appears to deserve the appellative "river." Topography is closer to the aboriginal landscape. Overall, this section of the East River looks more like an arm of the sea than a river through a city, and if the shoreline up here as drawn on a map looks solid, it is only because cartographers must draw their lines somewhere.

Whitestone was not my longest row, but it would take me farther out from land than any previous. As usual, rising tension invoked my atavistic fantasies of the sea: drifting, creatures lurking under the hull, land slipping farther away, the taste of salt. Was I in shape? If not, it was too late to do anything about it. Tense, yes, but not paralyzed: I get in the boat with the learned drudgery of any competent sailor. My ambition is to take in the river, to let experience confirm or deny my book learning.

We leave the davit, headed across Hell Gate Basin toward the Hog Back, which is activating the water into a froth. As much as I would like to row right over it, it would be a witless thing to do. Joe points to the rocks: too chancy for these boats. Yes, as soundly as these Whitehalls are constructed, a wooden hull is a fragile thing, in our case, Al tells us, only a quarter-inch thick. No percentage in trying the rocks: all it takes is one bad hit, and you go the way of the *Hussar*: down. So we stay clear as we round the point and head into the channel. Nevertheless, we hit a sudden churning in the water, which bounces us around some but does no harm—typical Hell Gate ruckus, Puck rather than Scylla or Charybdis being the agent in charge. The channel too is bois-terous, and again comes the "hideous roaring" from Saturday-morning traf-fic on the Triborough. We pick up a swift current, three, maybe four knots, very favorable but requiring steady rowing necessary to maintain control. We pass the bluffs of Ward's Island and Astoria, move under the bridges. We pass the wastewater treatment facilities on Randall's and, on the opposite shore, at the turn east toward the Sound, the Lawrence Point Generating Station, a massive facility of towers and electric generators. Ahead are the Brother islands, North and South. So disoriented is my sense of direction up here that it appears the brothers are adjacent east and west, but actually they are north and south, and as we pass they seem to slide into each other, becoming one leafy brushy occlusion against the background.

But first, a side trip to Steinway Creek. Past Lawrence Point we make an immediate turn to starboard hugging the shore of rip-rap. We move further into the inlet—Steinway Creek is one of its names, Luyster is another—a small stream emptying into Bowery Bay, which empties into the East River. Surrounding us are the generating station and another wastewater treatment plant, giant facilities harboring secret activity, hoses rigged to pumps at dock-side, blue flames from the tops of pipes burning gases from tanks. No humans

in sight. Signs at the waterside, their messages a cautionary ode: DANGER-
OUS CARGO/NO VISITORS/NO SMOKING/NO OPEN LIGHTS.
Nothing moves save some giant whirring fans that we can see in the ceiling
of a massive steel structure, a modernist industrial gazebo. These structures,
so carefully conceived and built, all have meaning down to the last pump
and bolt, but what meaning each has and how each thing fits into the total
design is lost on me. In the aggregate, they are used to process something—
process, in that generic sense when detailed activity is unknown, machines
to bring in source material, do something with it, and output another form
or another thing. Past the industrial facilities, we move into a more primeval
environment: riverbanks of dirt and junk rock, narrow and winding. We stop
for a break, and I plunge my oar into the water to take a reading—a depth-
sounding method I learned from some crew members. About four feet—
the color of the oar handle changes from ash to black, dripping black water,
sludge from the oily sediment. I clean off the sludge in the water, but the oil
residue remains, scarring the handle.

Old pictures of Bowery Bay and Steinway Creek show stock, sentimental
scenes, sepia rural: a stream, thin reeds, small boats tied to old docks. There's a
wow factor in these old pictures: you mean this place once looked like that? Yes,
and it still does, if you squint: a collapsed wooden structure, an old dock maybe
with an iron T-bar pushed upward through its deck (an old ship?). Steinway
Creek is about where a proposed canal was to be dug early on in the Gate's commercial history. To provide a way around the rocks at Hell Gate, some enter-
prising merchants and developers proposed in 1832 a canal through Astoria,
behind Hallett's Point, to link the upper East River with the lower. Given the
success of the recent Erie Canal and the pitch of canal fever still high, it was
feasible. But perhaps it would have been outdated even before it became opera-
tional, good for barges and lighters, but not for the ships that would soon be plying the Gate. Forward thinking but not forward enough, and nothing compared
to the plan—ambitious, crazed—of James Serrell a few decades later, in 1867.
Serrell—surveyor, engineer, fantasist—envisioned more than a mere canal. He
imagined an East River filled in (a favorite fantasy to this day of anyone who
crosses an East River bridge). Manhattan was to be fattened at the belly out to
about where 11th Street in Astoria is now. To the east of the new landfill, the
New East River, a canal essentially, dug straight, broad, and deep, without twists

and coves, without rocks and islands, a free-flowing ship channel from Bronx Kill to Wallabout Bay. And to the east of the New East River, a New New York, a suburb fitted with its own grid of grand boulevards and streets. A bold plan, visionary, fun to draw, impossible to achieve.

As we depart the creek—about the place where the west bank of the New East River would be, I'm thinking—we head back toward Lawrence Point. We slide in between the Brother Islands, North and South. South Brother to our starboard. The smaller of the two, it was once owned by Jacob Ruppert, Al tells us, the brewer and owner of the Yankees. You remember him. We take Al's words on faith because there is no sign of a house or ever one's existence here. Ruppert invited Babe Ruth over occasionally, and Babe, being the Babe, having nothing better to do at the East River, liked to show off by hitting golf balls from Ruppert's lawn far into the river.

North Brother, the larger island, still has tracings of its former self, one of those places whose renown is forgotten enough that it can be considered a secret of New York. Through the overgrown brush and the trees we can see abandoned buildings: hospitals, old military fortifications. A place of rumor and haunting: unspent ordinance is supposedly still scattered about. River-side Hospital. Here Typhoid Mary was confined and made her name, and here is the beach where the burned and drowned bodies from the *Slocum* were lined up. Can we put ashore and walk around a bit? Smell the forest and insects? See the old fortifications and brickwork, smell the desolation? No, not possible. No one is allowed on these islands now, except when accompanied by Parks people, but every so often a photographer sneaks on and takes captivating pictures of what nature does to the works of humankind. Squalor, moist and weathered brickwork, another waystation for birds on the Atlantic flyway. What to do with it? Nothing. Or else something. Proposals are floated every now and again. A park, some people think, would be nice. Every so often some genius has an idea to convert the island into a place of civic pride that might also bring in some money. Nothing as crass as an office park or a shopping center, but maybe a park with a purpose. One Bronx borough president proposed an amusement park, better than Disneyland, he said. I believe he was serious.

The Brothers straddle the deep-water channel. We row between them, keep an eye out for working vessels. None are visible from stem or stern. We are free for the moment to take in the sights, and to conjure ghost wrecks and victims. Coming through, we veer north a bit to put some distance between ourselves and Rikers Island, and just beyond that, LaGuardia Airport. Rikers Island was just another old rock, going back to the Dutch days, privately owned then and now city owned, an island of incarceration, sullen, gray, sad, infamous, and well policed, an icon mentioned in every cop show set in New York and therefore a national symbol. Come too close, and cop boats will appear from nowhere to shoo you away. Docked on the opposite shore is a huge boat that from a distance looks like a cruise ship waiting to pick up passengers, but it is actually an adjunct of the prison, the "prison barge."

It is a dull waste of landscape, the only point of interest being the planes that swoop overhead to land at LaGuardia, and I do mean *swoop*. Prevailing winds determine flight paths, and today's are unusual: planes coming from the north fly all the way west across the south Bronx and then at the last minute bank sharply, gull-like, to the south before descending precipitously to its designated runway. In the Dutch days, Rikers was an eighty-acre wasteland in the Oost Rivier. William Hallett, who had been appointed *schout*, or sheriff, of Flushing by Peter Stuyvesant, bought the island from the natives. That Hallett spent good money on such a nothing island angered Stuyvesant enough that he fired Hallett and gave the island away to a family named the Ryckens. They did nothing with it except lend their name. Much later, the island was used as an army base during the Civil War, a prison farm, a city dump and ash heap. Landfill, which expanded it over a few decades to more than four hundred acres. Ash and garbage were the main products here, and sometimes the resulting mounds (some one hundred feet or so in height) caught fire, appearing volcanic and phosphorescent, lighting up the night like Christmas, as a warden once described it. Rats were a problem; hunting parties were assembled—also dogs brought in and unleashed. Left to themselves, unfed and unfettered, they had to rely on the rats they caught for nourishment. The rats multiplied anyway. When he was planning his World's Fair in the late 1930s, Robert Moses did not want the hills of garbage and ash to loom as a backdrop to his carefully planned fairground at the head of Flushing Bay, so he had the dirt removed. Some of it went right next door to a small airport on the edge of the bay. Glenn Curtis Field at North Beach, it was called. Actually, the airport's beginnings happened because of its proximity to water:

seaplanes run by Pan American Airways were, at the time, the wave of the future. They landed right off shore before docking at Marine Air Terminal. The terminal is still in use, restored handsomely; photographs of the old seaplanes hang as curios on the wall of the cafeteria. It is now an adjunct to the airport next door, in the 1940s renamed LaGuardia, for the mayor. Before it was an airport, North Beach was a popular seafront, an amusement park with a Ferris wheel and restaurants, a wide beach. Recreation and summer getaways were the predominant uses for the whole East River shoreline, both sides between here and Throgs Neck. On the Bronx side, beach communities sprang up, small bungalows lining narrow lanes. Some still exist, now year-round residences, small pockets hidden from the interiors of the Bronx.

I could not help but think as we rowed farther east from Hell Gate that we were approaching the sea and its beginnings. I tried to put the city out of mind, not because it was madding and crowded, but because it was irrelevant. I preferred instead to focus on what needed attention now: rocks and islands and the smell of the sea. Water invites attention to the landscape, forces it. As I said, names like "East River" are something of a convention. One might consider this section of the river to be an arm of Long Island Sound. Adriaen Block's *Hellegat* opens wide: we are not on the sea, but for the first time I was wondering if I had to, could I swim to shore? I had no doubt I could, but neither did I want to be tested. The city dropped away to the edges of our horizon, and at the edges is a city of salt mounds, sand mounds, buildings with conveyors declining to the mounds, warehouses, trailer trucks. Emptying into the East River from the Bronx is the Bronx River, said with some exaggeration to be New York City's only true river, as it is a river and not a strait like the East and Harlem Rivers; and because both banks are within New York City perimeters, unlike the Hudson. But its source is farther north, in Westchester County, near Kensico and along its twenty-eight miles it drops over four hundred feet. If it has any fame at all it is because it flows through the middle of the Bronx, through the Bronx Zoo and near Fordham University. Like other marginal, semi-wild places, the Bronx River is an incipient scene of recreational activity, navigable by rowing craft up to a small waterfall, at which point you must turn back or else portage your vessel to continue. As we near its mouth I ask Joe if the outflow is going to hinder our progress. No, he says, it's an estuary, affected by the tides. And right now, the tide is going in. I forget how close we are to the sea. The eastern bank at its mouth is shrouded by trees running its length, and hidden behind them are warrens of the old bungalows. Further on is the mouth of Westchester Creek, like the Bronx River, thin and shallow once you get past its mouth.

Nautical charts denote wrecks in this part of the East River, most of which are the result of grounding: the water here is shallow, and the riverbed shifts owing to the incessant tidal movement. What wrecks remain are at the bottom, below our view, and most likely broken. But one curiosity remains above the water, just outside the mouth of Westchester Creek. We row toward it. It is ruined past the point of identification, its steel hull eroded and pocked with rusted holes. It has a pointed hull—beyond this, none of us (we are all amateurs at ship identification) can figure out what kind of ship it is (or was). We pull alongside—no markings, no name. Given its condition, it has been here maybe a few years, long enough to erode, not so long as to be reduced to pieces. Possibly a ferry of some kind—it is about the size of one. How did it get here? Grounding. How deep is the water? A crew member upends his oar and eases the butt end into the water, its blade barely showing. (This time no oily sediment.) About ten feet. Grounding, no doubt, explains the ship's location and abandonment—a navigational error on the part of the ship's pilot. No way should a ship this size be caught in water this shallow. Possibly an attempt to sneak into the harbor or an attempt to beat the system. Miscalculation or stupidity leads to many an accident. You would think that some agency would have been sent in the time hence to clear it, but then, why bother? It is outside the shipping channel and far enough from the creek's mouth so as not to be a hindrance to barges or other low-draft vessels that might enter.

It was later that I tried to research this wreck and piece together its story, but I could find few details, and what details there were made little sense. It seems that some entrepreneur from South America bought the boat and had it brought to the United States. His plan was to refurbish it and open it as a restaurant (the dream of many a New Yorker, especially those from out of town). Supposedly he intended to dock it in Philadelphia. One might suppose that he would finish the refurbishing in New York rather than Philadelphia and, further, that the facilities were somewhere in the East River or along Long Island Sound. Its bow was pointing west when we found it, meaning it was sailing in from Long Island Sound. Or else it got turned around in bad weather. One can guess and invent. The one truth is that it will remain where it is, as it is, until the water degrades it and renders it into unidentifiable chunks of rusted steel, yet another episode of bad weather or inept navigation to be forgotten. We cross the river from the Bronx side to the Queens side, a short crossing, College Point and Flushing Bay to our starboard.

Queens: borough of neighborhoods and small towns, once independent villages connected by paths and pikes, farms along the way, glacial till and kettle—now gridded over so completely it is impossible to tell where one neighborhood ends and the next begins. Swamplands, many of which still exist in isolated pockets or great swaths. A whole series of bays and inlets—Hempstead Harbor, Manhasset Bay, Little Neck Bay—are wide mouthed and funnel deeply into the north shore of Long Island. The source of these bays are creeks and ponds originating deep within Long Island. At low-tide, dark mudflats extend out from shore, the inlets that feed them darker still, winding through stretches of tall reeds—Phragmites, invasive and choking out other species. The wetlands of Flushing Bay once extended south to Union Turnpike and northeast into College Point, rendering College Point a peninsula at high tide. Encroachment narrowed and hemmed them. The swamps of Flushing Meadow (below Flushing Bay) eventually became the ash heaps and dumps made famous by F. Scott Fitzgerald in *The Great Gatsby*, until cleared by Robert Moses for the 1939 World's fair. Moses dammed Flushing Creek—to prevent the waters from the East River from flowing in, and in the process created two small lakes: Meadow Lake to the north and Willow Lake to the south. The lakes became part of the fair, and later the 1964 fair—water shows, grandstands, paths.

Now they are part of Flushing Meadow Park, recreational areas: kayaks and paddleboats for rent, sailing instructions. No swimming allowed. Meadow Lake is a moss green, surrounded by summertime grasses, tall enough in places to obscure the view across the lake. Some cattails, what look like daffodils. Ducks are active on shore, and appear healthy, quacking, feathery but dirty looking, dropping their heads in the water to feed on who knows what. Islands of scum floating in nearby puddles. We think of places like this as "wetlands." Once while walking along Meadow Lake, I thought to myself: I never see any fishermen in this lake. At that moment I saw a fisherman. I asked him if he had caught anything. Something small, he said, and threw it back. "They say," he told me, "there are bass and trout in here." "Ever caught one?" "Nope."

The GAIA Institute proposed in 2002 (for the 2012 Olympics) its plan to restore Flushing Meadows to a proper wetland: replacing underground culverts with open ponds to allow natural filtration by sunlight; varying shorelines—creating coves, essentially, and dredging bottom depths to increase the number of habitats needed for a more varied ecosystem. The 2012 Olympics went elsewhere, the GAIA plan nowhere. Local residents return. Pastoral in this city is where you find it.

Whitestone: Hilly, deep-set coves, pockmarked with kettles, carved by the ice sheets from the last ice age and smoothed over by succeeding millennia of warmth and wind and rain. Whitestone got its name from the limestone exposed on this peninsula of the north shore—a not so unusual geological phenomenon that could not help but draw attention to itself, a landmark then in the imaginations of the people who settled and traversed the area, hence a name. There exists a photograph of a large glacial erratic, white, and it is this white stone that is said to be the one. Francis Lewis owned an estate here, hence his name affixed to a park and a boulevard. Then a wealthy enclave, exclusive, neo-Newport, and since the early 20th century, when suburban development came here, a more modest neighborhood, housing open to the public.

It is just on the other side of the Bronx-Whitestone bridge that we will land. Tug and barge units appear—row harder!—sailboats, power boats— and we dodge them. My back starts to ache somewhere around the Bronx River, but worse are my hands, sore and calloused from gripping wooden oars. Stupidly, I had forgotten my gloves. I curse my skin and my stupidity. But we pass under the bridge and turn to starboard and make for the beach, rolling with the waves. We disembark, stretch our cramped bodies. We pull the boat far up on the sand. Trips to the bathroom. Then a look around: Phil was right in his lay of the land: a nice park sloping upward from the river, grass, a playground—residential, no stores within eyeshot. We sit in the park at picnic tables and open our packs. My lunch is a sandwich packed and crushed from being squeezed inside a backpack amid water bottles, sunscreen bottles, my notebook, a windbreaker in case the weather on the water is cold and stowed deeply within because it is not cold. We were explorers on break. Waiting for the tide to turn, we tour an enclave called Malba, hemmed in by

Powell Cove and the Bronx-Whitestone on-ramp: small lots, noble middle-class houses with sweeping long views of bridge and river, narrow jetties of rip-rap stretching far into the water, a place to fish from or an edge to stand on. With plenty of time to kill before the trip home, we saunter along trim lawns, clean, curving streets, and I wonder how often this neighborhood is invaded by the small of the sea.

Eventually we regroup, mostly to loaf and loiter. Above us, a milky sky. Off-shore, a tug and barge unit passes serenely by. No one really wants to get back in the boat for the return, but we have no choice. We ready the boat, untie the lines from the cleat we had stuck deeply into the sand. We gather our gear and begin to shove ourselves off, bow first into the water. A few small waves turn the bow to one side, at an angle to the beach, the stern still aground so that the boat pivots. But the waves do not let up, and as the water begins to lift and float the stern, the pivoting worsens so that the boat is put parallel to shore. To straighten it, to point bow outward, is a struggle. Then come bigger waves, wakes from the passing barge several minutes ago finally reaching us. The boat lifts up and down, then suddenly washed by a wave crashing over its beam. We're swamped. All we have for bailers are two plastic gallon jugs, so it takes several minutes before we're able to put our drenched bodies back into the boat and finally shove off.

The trick of mind that says the return trip is always shorter than the outbound trip is in force: we are making excellent progress. I tick off the same places in reverse order, the bridge, the shipwreck, and so on. Once past Powell Cove, the hills begin to flatten. Out in the middle of the river, suddenly I realize how isolated this place is. The land on all sides is distant, the boat low enough in the water as to be unseen by anyone onshore. From the water, it is easy to lose your orientation; things feel different. Someone comments on the expanse and the resulting isolation. Together with the slowness of rowing and the silence of nothingness, "You get a different perspective," says Phil. Another trick of mind: as you pass by these inlets and islands, landforms seem to slip by. You notice the one thing about the water, the shifting of objects on land, the land itself, the objects moving across like a picture show, the world reduced to a set of horizontals, screens moving in and out. Objects onshore are moving, not us. It is easy to lose yourself in illusion: slipping and sliding. The ancient Greeks called these objects *planktoi*, "wanderer" . . .

the wandering rocks . . . myth germinating from reality. Episodes and stories come forth, spun from actual experience. The critic Stuart Gilbert wrote of the phenomenon in his book on James Joyce, and suggests the legend of the wandering or clashing rock is most likely based on an optical illusion caused by a ship's being carried by a "swift, though imperceptible, current" through an archipelago: ". . . a labyrinth of such rocks . . . that would appear to be moving towards them, as the current bore the ship in that direction." On all sides, islands, landmarks, slipping past one another, occluding one another.

And then, seemingly suddenly, our reality shifts: lines of barge units to the east, and the city written onto the river in buoy markers, rules of the road, traffic. Barges move faster than we do, and those coming up on our stern will catch us soon enough. We are in the middle of the channel—you get the fastest current in the middle. One unit in particular, a tug with three barges in tow, is gaining on us. Perhaps we should move over. The captain of the tug unit has a high perch, and from his height believes he is close enough to do us some damage. We hear a stern voice through a bullhorn: "Good place to be if you want to get yourselves killed!" Couldn't be more succinct. Small boats, in barge world, are called "speed bumps." Mary Nell tells of another row, another captain; she heard him talking over his radio to other units: "I see this big canoe ahead in the channel . . . a very big canoe . . . filled with organ donors." I think of Captain Brucato about now, and his warnings to small craft. His sarcasm, too: could it be him speaking to us right now? He has a scant view of small boats doing sloppy things, and I begin to fear for the tug not being able to stop as much as for ourselves not able to get out of the way. If a bad end were to come to this little comedy, no matter whose fault it is, as Captain Brucato says, the tug would get the blame—the tug is Goliath, and the rowboat an innocent wanderer. But we clear out in a hurry, managing even to get far enough so that its wake is a minor blip as it passes under our keel.

After that brief push, we get back into rhythm. Rowing is a kind of madness: get a good rhythm going, and you believe you can go forever. The wooden seat is hard, and if you have no padding under your butt you well feel the hardness. And I still don't have gloves . . . these delicate city-boy hands can't take the scraping of skin against wood, so I've opened up old wounds—blisters, callouses. Skin peeling, smeared blood. The oar looks like a crime scene. I wash my hands in the river and splash water over the heel of the oar. A piece of dried skin dangles. I bite it off, roll it around my tongue a bit, then spit it over the gunwale: a piece of me now one with the East River, perhaps soon to be fish food. Still a long way to go. The Bronx River to our starboard, LaGuardia ahead to port. Another airliner swoops across the sky, down and low.

Hell Gate ahead, still invisible around the corner from LaGuardia. We're a little late, missing maximum ebb, but still making an ebb swift enough in our favor. The wind, though, is also strong, and against us. You'd think the wind would have small effect on a rowboat, but face your oar blade into the wind and the oar is almost a sail. Getting through it requires some push. "Pull" is the command for the oar to push the boat: "stroke!" Follow stroke; maintain rhythm. Good time for a sea shanty, but none of us know any. Before we even see the Gate, we feel the current pulling us, and the wind against us. We thread the Brothers. Ahead, to our backs as rowers, is the Hell Gate Arch, and just behind is the Triborough. Welcome portals. We stay close to the shore at Randall's Island, out of the way. Here we hit a back eddy and force our way through. "Push!" yells Phil. A wake and its quick rebound chops the water. "Push! Keep rowing, people . . . pull . . . pull!" As cox, Phil is a tyrant, as all coxes must be if the boat is to get anywhere. Many things to see and react to: chops, wind, both current traffic and traffic ahead. Get too close to the seawall, and you risk snapping the oar blades. "Starboard row!" "Port hold water!" Commands are not alarms but calls for focus and strength. Under the bridges, the roar of traffic overhead, around Negro Point into the Basin . . . things begin to calm. A last long stretch, davit in sight, and we're home.

I don't know which is spookier, the ship traffic or the expanse of water, the lowness of our boat to the water or the bones entombed in the muck below. You get another perspective, as Phil said earlier. Of old definitions, too, and topography. Bright passage: a wide and open sky. *Gat*: a hole, an opening. Rentenaar: "low-lying," "creek mouths." Pools, depth. I try to map this terrain above Hell Gate to Adriaen Block's. Block carried *Hellegat* with him across the Atlantic. If Stokes is right that the geographer De Laet followed Block's course in his descriptions, east to west, then Block saw this section of the East River before he ever saw the concentrated whirlings of what we now call Hell Gate. Block crosses the Atlantic to Massachusetts, explores its coast, names places after the familiar objects back home: *Zuyder Zee, Staten Hoeck*. He keeps going, passes Buzzards Bay and enters Long Island Sound. The Sound opens wider as he goes, and then at about New Haven it begins to narrow, seems to converge steadily. Whoosh of water against hull, cries and whoops of birds, buzz of insects. Smell of the sea. On both sides, the land lies low, hilly, inlets and deep coves, one after the other, the land's profile thin, a horizontal line under an open sky. Off Connecticut and Westchester, and Long Island: islands, rocks, what his map will designate as *Archipelagus*. Block passes a narrow spit of rock jutting far out into the Sound from the land on the northern shore—Throgs Neck.

Hellegat applied to the whole stretch of the East River. Block's journals are supposedly lost, and De Laet, if he ever knew, doesn't say where Block was when the name *Hellegat* came to him—or whether it was triggered by sight or sound or smell or some by-gone configuration that reminded him of home. If *Hellegat* really means low and swampy—being both water and the terrain that defines it—this place, the western part of Long Island Sound and into the narrower strait we know as the East River, might be where the explorer made his claim. The distance between *Hellegat* and "Hell Gate" over the centuries was the distance between a stretch of terrain in Holland, one of many, and a mythical patch of New York water. One can imagine Adriaen Block, mariner, making his way downriver, passing creek mouths, cutting through whirlpools, recalling the waters back home, and thinking wearily: *yet another hellegat.*

Years ago, my friends and I drove out to the tip of Cow Neck, the peninsula on which the towns of Port Washington and Manhasset are situated, because at the end of a peninsula you can find the end of the world. I knew these towns well, having lived various stretches of my youth in both, but of the town at the tip of Cow Neck, Sands Point, I knew nothing at all. This is where the invisible rich lived. Sands Point and across the mouth of Manhasset Bay, the neck to the west is Kings Point—East Egg and West Egg. This was Gatsby territory, immense mansions occluded by stone walls, trees, iron gates. It was possible in those days to drive to an outer point and clamber out on rocks by the thin strip of sand. As we pulled our car off the side of the road and strode out to the beach, suddenly in front was the ringlet of lights on the Throgs Neck Bridge: the entry to the city, the city that was far away on the Long Island Railroad. From here, the city appeared to be close by, its detail only a few short strokes away. Not far to the north, City Island was in view, and nearby, Hart Island, today's potter's field. At the end of *Gatsby,* Fitzgerald puts a reflective and moody Nick Carraway on a lawn overlooking the water to muse on the subject of arrivals and after: how it is that things went so wrong since the Dutch arrived and first laid eyes on what Fitzgerald sensuously characterized as the "green breast of the New World." The green breast of the New World . . . the East River? Hell Gate?

CHAPTER 8

Zeeland

Scylla and Charybdis

I imagine places to be *sentient beings*—Poe's term—that a place has properties or qualities peculiar to it, that it lives if not acts, has a temper, holds its own as a place amongst all places. Once when rowing down the East River channel heading for the Gate, a police boat coming from the Gate, seeing our direction, slowed and pulled up not far off our starboard. An officer stepped out on deck and warned us through his bullhorn to stay away from the Gate: "It's really ripping today." We were positioned in the east channel between Ward's Island and Manhattan, just north of the footbridge at 103rd Street. We had planned to enter the Gate but were calculating that we might not have time, and it was at that moment of indecision that the police boat intervened. The policeman did not order against continuing, but his warning gave us the excuse we were looking for. Just beyond the footbridge, to the south and around the bend of Ward's Island was the Gate, a vague and immense entity, and now after hearing the officer's warning, one at this moment in bad humor, surly. No matter that in a couple of hours, it would be dull and sluggish, and for the five or six minutes of slack tide, dead. Charybdis: the sea gets the last laugh; when Hurricane Sandy hit, it hit with a vengeance. Hell Gate Bay flooded, the sea took back the lowlands. Cellars filled with water. Downtown, the East River rose over the manmade bulwarks and flooded streets. For those hours, it created a new shoreline several blocks inland, just about where the original shoreline was.

I am this close to investing the place with spirits, as did the American Romantics, Irving and Cooper and Poe, who wrote of the place as though it were an animate thing: Irving's snoring aldermen, for example, and for that

we can blame the English name of the place: Hell Gate. I had seen Hell Gate
several times when young, before knowing it was *Hell Gate*. I saw it through
the window of the family Plymouth while cruising along the East River Drive,
although I did not know *East River Drive*. It was night, we were driving somewhere—an aunt and uncle lived in Italian Harlem—but were we on our way
there or on our way home? What I do remember are the lights, whose blue
beams, straight and rhythmic as oars, passed through the windshield and to
the backseat, from where I observed. I made a transient home for myself back
there; I did this in whatever space I found myself in. Through the window, I
viewed a wide body of water whose surface was stilled, calm enough to reflect
the blue, red, orange, and white city lights with no distortion. Slack tide on
the East River, though I didn't know the term "slack tide." How calm it was,
how calm I was, in the hole of the backseat on those trips. Every now and
again on our way into the city we'd cross the Triborough. A fear of bridges led
me to duck below, to climb off the backseat and hole up in the well where legs
are meant to be. Below me, below the underside of the car, below the roadway
and the steel bridge, was Hell Gate, of which I was not conscious. What I did
understand was the considerable height between me and the darkness, and
whatever else was below: the black water, the green shores, the nothingness.

From the seawall at Ward's Island, the city is close but far away because
here the city is without noise. The city is plainly visible, but the cars and
trucks tool by as though on a silent conveyor belt, small objects with no obvious sign of control other than the belt on which they are positioned whose
invisible mechanism pulls them along. The buildings behind are walls with
arrays of windows, uninhabited. The city is a crenellated wall designed to fool
strangers who approach into thinking that here the city is quiet. Spanning the
Hell Gate channel are two bridges: the Triborough and the Hell Gate Arch
Bridge. Both are segments of transportation systems that extend far beyond
the limits of Hell Gate.

The Hell Gate Arch Bridge is the more beautiful of the two in a La Belle
Époque sort of way, a bowstring arch between two towers sheathed in stone—
unnecessary ornament from an engineering point of view, mere pleasantries
to the eye. It was designed to be a handsome portal to ships arriving from
the northeast, City Beautiful in its wane, and yet the eye is pleased. Of the
two bridges, it was the first to be built, in 1916, the sole span over the Gate,

the design of Swedish engineer Gustav Lindenthal. It was but one node of
a system conceived by Alexander Cassatt, president of the Pennsylvania
Railroad, who decided he wanted a direct route into and out of Manhattan.
His objective was to compete with Cornelius Vanderbilt, whose New York
Central was able to come directly into Manhattan from the north and stop
at Grand Central Terminal, at 42nd Street. So Cassatt embarked on his own
project to one-up Vanderbilt. His system included a tunnel from New Jersey
into Manhattan, a continuation underground all the way through the tender-
loin of Manhattan, Pennsylvania Station at 34th Street and Seventh Avenue,
a tunnel under the East River, the Sunnyside Yards in Long Island City, the
Hell Gate Bridge, the rest of the viaduct above Ward's and Randall's Islands,
and more miles of track into the Bronx. Quite a project. I connected with it
myself in my small way, a boy living in Astoria, watching the diamond-backed
trains speeding along the viaduct on its way to the Hell Gate Arch, at the time
ignorant of that fact and anything other than the train's power and speed and,
above all, its snare-drum staccato rhythm.

The Triborough, further south, was another brainchild of Robert Moses,
who wanted to advance cars and highways. It is a tri-part complex: a suspen-
sion bridge over the channel; a truss bridge connecting Randall's Island to the
Bronx, and a vertical-lift bridge connecting Randall's Island to Manhattan. It
neatly connects three boroughs: Manhattan, Queens, and the Bronx, its name
thus a perfect reflection of its function. Now, renamed for Robert Kennedy,
its appellation no longer suggests its geography. These two bridges, parallel
to and only a few hundred yards from each other, together reflect a dyadic
nature: the superimposition of the Triborough's descending catenary cables
against the rising bow-arch of the Hell Gate.

There are no signs, no markers on any of its walks or esplanades to indicate
that here is Hell Gate, and the two bridges serve to transform Hell Gate in
another way: by rendering it invisible to those who pass over it. A bridge, no
matter its serviceability or its intrinsic beauty negates what flows underneath
by spanning it, overcoming it. That of course is its purpose. As land transportation increased in importance, and bridges were built, it made travel easier
and practical. Commuters, ignorant of what is below, become frequent flyers,
Hell Gate's metaphorical stature as a portal lost to most. But for those who
walk its edges or challenge its currents, it remains an inner sea.

Floating

Low water, slack tide, water gray as slate, dark thick band of waterstain along Mill Rock, water still and deceptive as a mudflat.

South from the seawall, a meticulous construction of granite and mortar: the bottle-nosed northern tip of Roosevelt Island is flattened, pressed into the body, its beam wide and pointing straight at you.

The Parabola Building is full faced but squat, something less than itself surrounded by the immeasurable city of walls behind it.

Traffic continues silently on the drive.

From the seawall: rocks poking above the surface, capped with lamps; buoys with bells dinging.

Hiss of foam.

Sing-song of subaqueous creatures.

Painted in whitewash on a gray granite block: *NIKE*, honoring . . . ? The winged goddess? The missile? Or the sportswear?

What do I here?

Chase a few names, attend images, track terrain. All in a day's pleasure. The name Hell Gate is loaded with contraries: the river that is not a river, the currents that flow both ways, the two bridges, the imagery of bright passage and hell hole. Whether heaven or hell or a low-lying swampy place is a test of outlook. Elusiveness renders the place a paradox: Hell Gate might frustrate meaning, or might be a vehicle to hold ambiguity, ambivalence.

Looking for the bottom of meaning—the root cause—is an American pastime. The American romantics in their interpretation of Hell Gate concentrated on the *helle*: "bright" or "hell." The Dutch seemed to consider it just another *gat* in a coastline of *gats*, like the many back home: low, earthy, watery, and unspectacular. Where myth meets earth and water. "Bright passage" or "hell hole": even if *hellegat* is not invested with these meanings, the ambivalent image has come down through the years: paradise thwarted by reality, bafflement, contraries, erupting violence.

On modern nautical charts, the old names are still written, and they're still used in the radio calls of mariners as well, which makes them extant in the minds of speakers: Hogback, Hallett's, Brothers, and Negro Point. When Henry Stern, the former Parks commissioner, discovered this name, Negro

Point, for the southeastern corner of Ward's Island, he found it offensive. The origin of the name is not clear, but it has appeared on charts before anyone can remember. Captain Brucato passed on to me a story he once heard—true or not, he was unsure—that Negro Point was named after an African American who helped a British warship. No doubt this was the *Hussar*, and the African American was Swan. If true, this gives the name historical significance, but also a political problem, which the commissioner decided to correct, suggesting instead that it be renamed Scylla Point. This would stand as a neat counterpoint to the Charybdis Playground in Astoria Park located directly across the channel. Scylla Point harked back to the classics, and it was Stern's intent to invoke this classic history. But in 2011, the U.S. Geographic Board of Names (there actually is a group that rules on toponyms) rejected the name Scylla Point. (Google maps displays Scylla Point on its map of Ward's Island, apparently unaware that the nautical charts and the mariners still use its old name.) The image of Scylla and Charybdis comes easily, but its actuality here is more benign than in the ancient world: playgrounds instead of monsters.

The placidness of water is an attraction, and so is immersion. A body this far from drowning. Every so often, police boats can be seen searching for something in the water. A rumor spreads that two nights earlier someone jumped off the footbridge at 103rd Street. If so, the search boats might be looking in the wrong place; that body could be anywhere between the Long Island Sound and Coney Island by now. But just as likely, it has been shunted back and forth and has returned to the point where the living person hit the water.

The historian and minister Daniel Van Pelt considered the two natures in the received interpretations of *Hellegat*, claiming it meant hell and reasoning that *hell* had been confused with the German word for bright. He lived nearby, in Astoria, and made it a habit to go down to the Gate at night to bathe in its invigorating waters. One night he could be heard yelling for help, but nothing was, or could be, done for him. His clothes were found neatly folded on a rock just offshore. Several days later, his drowned body was found washed up on the shore of the Narrows, at the mouth of New York Harbor, Bay Ridge, Brooklyn.

One spring afternoon while leaning on the rail, I watched the usual parade of sailboats, cabin cruisers, cigarette boats, and catamarans coming down from the Gate, all of them under power against the flood tide coming upriver.

One after the other continued on, but oddly, they all came to a stop about twenty blocks or so downriver, off the East Sixties, gathering as if at the start of a race. Their engines cut, they all began to drift north in the direction they came from. As they drifted upriver, they formed a circle about some object, and as they got closer still, I could make out that the object of their interest was a small, brownish object drifting in the water, a piece of canvas or something, its wet surface glinting in the sunlight. This piece of flotsam drifts as the currents take it, and the boats are merely moving with it, keeping a distance from it, what seems to be a *respectful* distance. As they got closer still, I saw that the object was not a piece of canvas at all, but a brown jacket on the back of a body, face down, arms splayed: the dead man's float they call it when the living do it. Bodies drowned in winter fill with gas as the water and air warm, and then float to the surface. He floated past John Finley Walk and up around Horns Hook, the flotilla of pleasure boats still in his company. Finally, a police boat showed up and put itself in the middle of the flotilla, parking itself adjacent to the body to haul it in with grappling poles: poles designed for the purpose of plucking flotsam from the water. Even after the police took over, the flotilla and the thin crowd of us on shore that followed along remained, no longer out of sense of guardianship but from curiosity and dread. One imagines the last spark of a life being the knowledge of its imminent end. Melville characterized his isolato Bartleby figuratively: "a bit of mid-Atlantic wreckage." Here it was literal, a man become a body, floating with the current along with everything else that floats. Bodies in water bloat, and I would not second guess the coroners, but bloating is not what I saw. I saw stiff limbs, arms extended outward from the body, almost as though the body were about to draw a weapon from a holster, a hand jutting from a jacket sleeve. Rigor mortis had set in, and as the body was pulled out of the water and suspended in mid-air, it was for that moment a stark, blackened thing: driftwood. Someone would later get the news. Surely someone knew the man who had inhabited the body. I learned nothing of the end of this story, nor its beginning.

On the Perimeter Road

Out here along the perimeter road, which follows the edge of Tenkenas are small and transitory settlements. All highways lead here. Caravans have been arriving since morning from outlying parts of the city, converging here to escape the city, the joy of escaping, which is a state of mind. The caravans drive slowly, the drivers surveying the surroundings for a patch of land big enough to accommodate their party and on which they can stake a claim, near the water's edge or otherwise. When the driver and the elders of the party agree on a place, they stop: hocus locus, this is the place. Synthetic pastoral: grassy knolls, granite boulders, the calming effect of a river. The travelers alight and begin to unload the goods they have brought, stowing them on the grass in neat piles. Each traveler has his or her own task, tasks arranged beforehand so that no questions need be asked. The men do the heavy lifting, and the women arrange the chairs and blankets; those too young to assist are told to stay close but out of the way. Ice coolers are set on the ground alongside meat wrapped in plastic bags, cases of soda and beer, fishing gear.

Each settlement is defined by a circle of chairs. On the chairs sit women and girls and in and out between them scoot their children. At the perimeter of the circle a small fire is to be built and tended carefully. All these are settlements for the day only, built for outings lasting the whole day and no more than the day. Each is impregnable, but none is a fortress. What keeps strangers out is not a battalion of arms but common courtesy, the recognition of a right to stake a claim and the expectation that no trespass will be done. A village built on a single principle. Inland, it is farming. Out here by the sea, it is fish. Those that are caught become part of the meal.

The cook begins to build his fire. An honored ritual: charcoal dumped into the grill pit, drenched with fluid, a match lit and thrown. Flames rise and dance. The cook and the children at his side watch. Everyone clusters in the chairs and on blankets, and when the fire settles into a low smolder, the cook takes his place in a chair. Meanwhile, everyone talks, jokes, laughs. Music from radios is played loud because everyone wants to hear it.

Wanderers pass the settlements along the perimeter road. Most pass through, stopping along the way to admire the sea. Some stop to engage the settlers. They might be invited into the circle, but more often only friendly greetings are exchanged and the wanderers continue on their way.

A wanderer by the seawall ventures too close to a fisherman about to cast a line. Someone yells out, "Stay back!" and scolds: "You don't want a hook in your eye, do you?" "No," says the wanderer, meekly. He didn't know the rules.

A fisherman catches a striper. I know it's a striper because he says it's a striper, and he knows it's a striper because, as he says, "it has no fight in him." He lifts it up and places it on the ledge of the seawall. "There's something wrong here," he says, meaning the fish is too small to be eaten. He removes the hook and throws the fish back into the river. "Tell your grandfather to come next time," he says to the fish. "Tsk," says another fisherman to me in private as he passes by. "I eat what I catch."

What is this place, the philosopher's road?

Wanderers stop each other to talk, to kill time.

The currents funnel here, through the channel. The channel is whitewater, rough and raucous. Fishing is good in whitewater, but here it is sometimes troublesome. There he is: a fisherman trying to make a go of it, and he is in something of a jam. At the end of his line something is tugging, his rod a graceful arc, his taut line extending far into the channel, his face a register of nerves. He looks up at me watching him as though I'm his audience, which in fact I happen to be at this moment. Wanderers find themselves gathering together, lured by *events*—the perimeter road is well traveled. Some linger, anticipating the fisherman's struggle will turn into a small drama. When you have nowhere to be, small dramas make good sideshows. A burly man comes by with a woman and, seeing the trouble, begins to move through the gathering crowd toward the fisherman, as though he is going to save him. He is hugeness and noise, the showman of fishing who will loudly instruct others on how things are to be done. "You've got to be careful," he says. "they dart up and down between the rocks." He means the fish. He talks like an expert. "I know these rocks." He has fished here himself, apparently, and has come to understand the currents and the rocks hidden beneath well enough that they are another room in his imagination.

He offers to take the rod, which the fisherman extends and passes to him. The expert tugs gently, walks a few steps this way, then the other way. Nothing comes of this, it is all show, and he returns the rod to the fisherman. "You've got something there," the expert laughs: "an old tire!"

Cars pull up and stop; people get out. Bicyclists, walkers, all who come by now stop to watch, or else to act. Someone helps the fisherman steady the rod while he reels in the line. Music comes from a car radio. Someone cranks up the volume. A couple of girls begin to move in time. By now, a party is developing at the fringes of the crowd—music, dancing. But there is work to be done. Some of the men help the fisherman haul in the line, the expert included. They take turns manning the rod, but there is no movement, no progress . . . the workings of genius appear as torment and insanity to angels, wrote William Blake. Boredom seeps in, girls check their fingernails, people study shoes. The reeling becomes easy, far too easy. This is not progress, this is the end. "Aaagh!" cries the expert. "I told you you've got to be careful!" Bully talk, not expertise. But he has seen the inevitable before anyone else: the line has broken. The audience begins to dissipate. The fisherman packs it in, and one must admire his courage—the courage not to say I will be back, but to say instead *I am done.*

The fisherman says, "I'm done."

No bravado, no melodrama. No tension: the line has broke.

At the seawall now, the river is calm, at slack tide. A strange configuration: stuck in the ground are four identical fishing poles, each about fifteen feet tall, spaced about forty feet apart. Around the base of each are small cairns of rocks, presumably to bolster the poles and keep them erect. Each pole has a thin line extending from its tip almost invisibly far out into the water. Together, they are a precise construction, and seem to be the work of a single individual or maybe a small group who act as one. What is most strange is that no one is in attendance. Most poles are manned or have someone nearby. Not these. They appear to be a unified work conceived, erected, and then abandoned, something left behind for later generations to come across and ask, "What is it? Who built it? Why did they leave?"

The nearest party to these poles is a family resting on a blanket in the shade under a tree. Maybe they are in charge. Or not. None pays any mind to the poles. Nevertheless, I give them credit for the construction, if only for their proximity to it and a small box of fishing tackle I see near their blanket. This is their home for the afternoon: the blanket marks their plot of land, all their possessions within reach. The man is lying on his back, his wife lying next to him, her head resting on his chest. They appear to be asleep, but perhaps they are only resting with their eyes closed. Their two girls sit cross-legged at the foot of the blanket, playing cards. One looks to be about eight or nine, the other about six. The older seems bored, impatient. Perhaps she is losing their little game, or maybe she is only entertaining her younger sister because she has been told to. She slaps down a card.

Go fish, Christ tells Peter, fisherman, fisher of men, and I think of the puns and inside jokes that helped found a religion, transforming the ordinary into myth: Peter = *petros* = rock . . . upon this rock. And I C H T H Y S . . . *Iesous Christos Theou Yios Soter* = Jesus Christ, Son of God, Savior = *ichthys* = fish. The fisherman and his wife can't be bothered with juvenile argument. It's the weekend, and both are reposed in private, unspeaking communication. The fisherman never once raises his head to eye his lines. Perhaps he doesn't need to. The poles are solidly placed, staked securely in the ground. If he's lucky, something will stir. The couple seem detached from all that surrounds them. But the place is tricky, moody: a change in the water might make a difference. The poles are the antennae, the bites the signal.

ACKNOWLEDGMENTS

A few mates and guides: Andy Pirone, for his stories of the neighborhood and local history; Marco Gonzalez, for clueing me in on fishermen and their habits of mind; Marie Lorenz, who gave me my first opportunity to row on the East River (in a rowboat of her own design and construction); the staff at the Long Island City Boathouse; Richard Melnick and Bob Singleton, of the Greater Astoria Historical Society, for their vast knowledge of Hell Gate and the East River; Bill Brucato of Reinauer Transportation, from whom I learned about modern navigation through Hell Gate; David Karabell, of the Central Park Conservancy, who served as my guide through the park's North Woods and for his knowledge of New York landscape and history; Christopher Girgenti, of Randall's Island Park Alliance, for his guidance through the natural history of the Bronx Kill; various members of the NYC Parks Department, including John the gardener.

This book would have been very different if not for my rowing mates at the East River Crew: Tori Gilbert, Phil Yee, Mary Nell Hawk, Al Stashin, Joe Herrod, Ismael Figueroa, Katherine Winkleman, Therese Sullivan, and Steve Villaverde.

Also, my thanks to the staff of the New York Public Library Map Room; to Lauren Robinson of the Museum of the City of New York; to Tamara Rafkin, for advice and help with Dutch translations; to Matt Kania for his maps of Hell Gate and the East River; to Elaine Elinson, who read an early draft of this book; and to Amanda Lanne-Camilli of SUNY Press for shepherding this project.

Credits

Parts of this work have appeared in a different form in Gotham History Blotter, 2012, Gotham Center for New York City History.

Detail from the Figurative Map of Adriaen Block, 1614, p. 11. The Miriam and Ira D. Wallach Division of Art, Prints, and Photographs; Print Collection, New York Public Library.

Hell Gate Ferry Hotel, Eliza Greatorex, p. 26; Museum of the City of New York.

Gracie Mansion, Eliza Greatorex, p. 31; Museum of the City of New York.

Hell Gate, 1830s, Archibald L. Dick, p. 70 Museum of the City of New York

Detail from the 1851 Survey of Hell Gate, p. 78: National Oceanic and Atmospheric Administration.

BIBLIOGRAPHY

Baard, Erik. "Uneasily Evoking an Outdated Past." *New York Times*, July 8, 2001.

Badhe, Thomas. "The Common Dust of Potter's Field: New York City and its Bodies Politic, 1800–1860." *Common-place: The Interactive Journal of Early American Life* 6(4), July 2006. www.common-place.org

Bancroft, George. *History of the United States of America*. New York: D. Appleton & Co. 1886.

Blackwell, David. Lecture at the Greater Astoria Historical Society, December, 2008.

Blesh, Rudi. "Scott Joplin: Black-American Classicist." 1971. In *Scott Joplin: Complete Piano Works*. Vera Brodsky Lawrence, ed. Miami: CPP/Belwin, 1981.

Bradford, William. *Of Plymouth Plantation*. Harvey Wish, ed. New York: Capricorn Books, 1962.

Brewer, E. Cobham. *Dictionary of Phrase and Fable*. 1870. Reprinted: New York: Avenel Books, 1978.

Brodhead, John Romeyn. *History of the State of New York*, Vol. 2. New York: Harper and Brothers, 1871.

Brucato, Bill. "New York City's East River and Hell Gate." May 17, 2009. *New York Tugmaster's Weblog*. Retrieved from captbbrucato.wordpress.com/2009/05/17/new-york-citys-east-river-and-hell-gate

Bulfinch, Thomas. *Mythology*. Abridged. Edmund Fuller, ed. New York: Dell, 1959.

Burrows, Edwin, and Mike Wallace. *Gotham: A History of New York City to 1898*. New York: Oxford University Press, 1999.

Caro, Robert. *The Power Broker*. New York: Random House, 1975.

Cooper, James Fenimore. *The Water-Witch, or, the Skimmer of the Seas; a Tale*. New York: Hurd and Houghton, 1872. In *Making of America*, University of Michigan and Cornell University; Ann Arbor: University of Michigan Library, 2005.

Crapsey, Edward. "The Nether Side of New York." *The Galaxy*, Vol. XI, No. 3, March, 1871. In *Making of America*, Ithaca, NY: Cornell University Library,1999–2009.

Cutter, William R. *Genealogical and Family History of Southern New York and the Hudson River Valley*. New York: Lewis Publishing, 1912.

Danckaerts, Jasper. *Journal, 1679–1680*. Bartlett Burleigh James and J. Franklin Jameson, eds. New York: Charles Scribner's Sons, 1913.

Davenport, W.H. "Blackwell's Island Lunatic Asylum," *Harper's New Monthly Magazine*, February 1866, Vol. 32, No. 189. In *Making of America*. Ithaca, NY: Cornell University Library, 1999–2009.

Denton, Daniel. *A Brief Description of New York: Formerly Called New Netherlands*, London, 1670. In Lincoln Libraries and University of Nebraska, Lincoln, Electronic Texts in American Studies. Paul Royster, ed., 2006.

Finley, John. "Traveling Afoot." *The Art of Walking*. Edwin Valentine Mitchell, ed. New York: Vanguard Press, 1948.

Fitzgerald, F. Scott. *The Great Gatsby*. New York: Charles Scribner's Sons, 1925.

Folsom, George, ed. "Translations from the Latin and French Editions of De Laet's New World; 1633–1640." *Collections of the New-York Historical Society, Second Series*, Vol. 1. New York: H. Ludwig, 1841.

GAIA Institute. *Ecological Engineering and Restoration Study: Flushing Meadow Lakes and Watershed*. June, 2002. Retrieved from www.thegaiainstitute.org /Gaia/Flushing%20Meadows%20Lakes%20and%20Watershed%20Restoration _files/Gaia%20Institute%20Ecological%20Engineering%20and%20Restoration %20Study-%20Flushing%20Meadows%20Lakes%20and%20Watershed.pdf

Gilbert, Stuart. *James Joyce's Ulysses: A Study*. New York: Random House, 1955.

Greatorex, Eliza, and Despard, Matilda. *Old New York: From the Battery to Bloomingdale*, Vol. 2. New York: G. P. Putnam's Sons, 1875.

Guiterman, Arthur. *Ballads of Old New York*. New York: Harper Bros., 1920.

Hassett, Maurice. "Symbolism of the Fish." *The Catholic Encyclopedia*. Vol. 6. New York: Robert Appleton Company, 1909. Retrieved from www.newadvent.org /cathen/06083a.htm

Homer, *The Odyssey*. Robert Fagles, translator. New York: Penguin Books, 2006.

Irving, Washington, *Tales of a Traveller*, 1824 (Library of America edition, New York, 1991.)

Jackson, Kenneth T., ed. *The Encyclopedia of New York City*. New Haven, CT: Yale University Press, 2010.

Jameson, John Franklin, ed. "From the 'New World,' by Johan de Laet." *Narratives of New Netherland, 1609–1664*. New York: Charles Scribner's Sons, 1909.

Joyce, James. *Ulysses*. 1922. (New York: Modern Library, 1961.)

Kadinsky, Sergey. *Hidden Waters of New York City: A History and Guide to 101 Forgotten Lakes, Ponds, Creeks, and Streams in the Five Boroughs*. Woodstock, VT: Countryman Press 2016.

Kazimiroff, Theodore L. *The Last Algonquin*. New York: Walker and Company, 1982.

Kieran, John F. *A Natural History of New York*. Boston: Houghton Mifflin, 1959.

Kilgannon, Corey. "For Veteran Tug Captain, a Job That Runs in the Family Turns Deadly." *New York Times*, March 19, 2015.

King, Charles. "New York in 1809: Reminiscences of the Firm of Archibald Gracie & Company." *The Magazine of American History with Notes and Queries*, Vol. 3. John A. Stevens, ed. New York: A.S. Barnes, 1879.

Kornblum, William. *At Sea in the City*. Chapel Hill, NC: Algonquin, 2002.

Kouwenhoven, John A. *Columbia Historical Portrait of New York*. New York: Icon Editions / Harper & Row, 1972.

Library of Congress. "The Atlantic World: Dutch Place Names." Retrieved from frontiers.loc.gov/intldl/awkbhtml/kb-1/kb-1-2-5.html

Lofaso, Anthony. *Origins and History of the Village of Yorkville in the City of New York*. Bloomington, Indiana: Xlibris, 2010.

Lopate, Philip. *Waterfront*. New York: Random House, 2005.

Lossing, Benson J. *The Empire State*. Hartford, CT: American Publishing, 1888.

Maccoun, Townsend. "Manhattan Island, 1783, At the Close of the Revolution." Map, 1909. Author's collection.

Maeder, Jay. "Built like a Bonfire: General Slocum, 1904." *New York Daily News*, March 12, 1998.

Melville, Herman. *Moby Dick*, 1851. (New York: Bobbs-Merrill, 1964.)

Mines, John Flavel. *A Tour Around New York and My Summer Acre*. New York: Harper and Brothers, 1893.

The New International Encyclopedia, vol. 9. New York: Dodd, Mead and Company, 1908.

New York City Department of Correction History. "1920 Scenes of Rikers Rising from the River." Retrieved from www.correctionhistory.org/html/chronicl /nycdoc/1920s-Rikers-landfill-photos/1920s-rikers-landfill-scenes-starter.html

New York Times. "The Confession of William Saul and Nicholas Howlett, concerning the Murder of Charles Baxter—Exculpation of Johnson." January 24, 1853.

———. "Rambling About Ward's Island: A Visit to Potter's Field." August 21, 1855.

———. "Revolutionary Wreck: *HMS Hussar*." September 8, 1856.

———. "Ward's Island, Its Ancient and Modern History." November 27, 1874.

———. "Killed on Ward's Island: A Lunatic Murdered by River Thieves." April 20, 1884.

NOAA Office of Coast Survey. "Chart 12339: East River (Tallman Island to Queensboro Bridge)." January, 2013. Retrieved from www.charts.noaa.gov/OnLineViewer /12339.shtml

O'Donnell, Edward T. *Ship Ablaze: The Tragedy of the Steamboat* General Slocum. New York: Broadway Books, 2003.

Pittsburgh Press. "Phantoms of the Sea: Tide Brings in Gruesome Corpse-Box with Its Weird Mystery." April 26, 1934. Google News Service. Retrieved from news .google.com/newspapers?nid=1144&dat=19340425&id=zEwbAAAAIBAJ& sjid=lksEAAAAIBAJ&pg=4148,3367048

Poe, Edgar Allan. "Doings of Gotham." *Columbia Spy*, 1844. In *Writing New York: A Literary Anthology*. Philip Lopate, ed. New York: Washington Square Press, 1998.

———. "A Descent into the Maelstrom." *Edgar Allan Poe: Poetry, Tales, and Selected Essays*. New York: Library of America, 1996.

Preble, George H. "Wreck of H.M. Frigate Hussar." *United Service Monthly Review of Military and Naval Affairs*, vol. XI. Philadelphia: L. R. Hamersly, 1884.

Rastorfer, Darl. *Six Bridges: The Legacy of Othmar H. Ammann.* New Haven, CT: Yale University Press, 2000.

Rattray, Jeanette Edwards. *Perils of the Port of New York.* New York: Dodd, Mead & Company, 1973.

Rentenaar, Rob. "Er is geen reden om bij Hell Gate aan Indiaanese afkomst te denken . . ." In David L. Gold, *Studies in Etymology and Etiology: With Emphasis on Germanic, Jewish, Romance and Slavic Languages.* San Vincente del Raispeig, Alicante, Spain: Publicaciones de la Universidad de Alicante, 2009.

Richardson, James. "The Unbarring of Hell Gate." *Scribner's Monthly*, Vol. 3, No. 1. New York, November, 1871. In *Making of America.* Ithaca, NY: Cornell University Library, 1999–2009.

Rockland County Journal. "Mr. Van Pelt Drowned." November 3, 1900. Southeastern New York Library Resources Council, 2015. Retrieved from news.hrvh.org /veridian/cgi-bin/senylrc?a=d&d=rocklandctyjournal19001103.2.6&srpos=0& e=-------en-20--1--txt-txIN-------#

Rogers, Heather. *Gone Tomorrow: The Hidden Life of Garbage.* New York: The New Press, 2005.

Ruttenber, E.M. "Footprints of the Red Men: Indian Geographical Names." *Proceedings of the New York State Historical Association, The Seventh Annual Meeting, With Constitution, By-Laws, and List of Members.* New York State Historical Association, 1906.

Sante, Luc. *Lowlife: Lures and Snares in Old New York.* New York: Farrar, Straus, Giroux. 1991.

Scherman, Katherine. *The Flowering of Ireland.* Boston: Little, Brown and Co., 1981.

Scoville, Joseph. *The Old Merchants of New York City*, Vol. 1. New York: Carleton, 1863.

Seitz, Sharon, and Stuart Miller. *The Other Islands of New York City: A History and Guide.* 3rd ed. Woodstock, VT: Countryman Press, 2011.

Steinberg, Ted. *Gotham Unbound: The Ecological History of Greater New York.* New York: Simon & Schuster, 2014.

Stern, Ellen. *Gracie Mansion.* New York: Rizzoli, 2005.

Stewart, George R. *Names on the Land.* New York, Random House, 1945 (New York: NYRB, 2008).

Stokes, I. N. Phelps. *The Iconography of Manhattan Island, 1498–1909.* New York: Robert H. Dodd, 1915–1928.

Tauranac, John. *Essential New York.* New York: Hold, Rinehart and Winston, 1979.

Ten Bruggencate, K. *Engels Woordenboek.* 17th ed. R.W. Zandvoort, J. Gerritsen, ed. Groningen, NL: H. D. Tjeenk Willink, 1974.

Tooker, William Wallace. *Indian Place-Names on Long Island and Islands Adjacent, With Their Probable Significations.* New York: G.P. Putnam's Sons, 1911.

———. *Indian Names of Places in the Borough of Brooklyn: With Historical and Ethnological Notes.* New York: F.P. Harper, 1901.

Tracy, Robert. "'All Them Rocks in the Sea': Ulysses as Immram." *Irish University Review* 32, no. 2. Edinburgh: Edinburgh University Press, 2002.

Van der Donck, Adriaen. *A Description of the New Netherlands.* Thomas F. O'Donnell, ed. Syracuse, NY: Syracuse University Press, 1968.

Van Pelt, Daniel. *Leslie's History of the Greater New York.* New York: Arkell Publishing Co., 1898.

Verdam, J. *Middelnederlandsch Handwoordenboek.* C.H. Ebbinge Wubben, ed. s'Gravenhage: Martinus Nijhoff, 1949.

Waldman, John. "The Harbor Nobody Knows." *New York Times,* Feb. 20, 2000.

Wilson, James Grant, ed. *The Memorial History of the City of New York: From Its First Settlement to the Year 1892,* Vol 4. New York: New-York History Co., 1893.

Winthrop, John. *A journal of the transactions and occurrences in the settlement of Massachusetts and the other New-England colonies, from the year 1630 to 1644.* Noah Webster, ed. Hartford: Elisha Babcock, 1790. In Evans Early American Imprint Collection. Ann Arbor, MI: Text Creation Partnership, 2004–12.

Wolfe, Gerard R. "Hell Gate." In *The Encyclopedia of New York City.* Kenneth Jackson, ed. New Haven, CT: Yale University Press, 2010.

WPA Guide to New York City. New York: Pantheon, 1982. (Originally published in 1939.)